Teaching Developmental Immigrant Students in Undergraduate Programs

A PRACTICAL GUIDE

Teaching Developmental Immigrant Students in Undergraduate Programs

A PRACTICAL GUIDE

By Myra M. Goldschmidt & Debbie Lamb Ousey

Ann Arbor
University of Michigan Press

ISBN-13: 978-0-472-03434-5

2014   2013   2012   2011   4   3   2   1

Foreword

by Cate Crosby, West Chester University of Pennsylvania

Currently, there is a growing population of language learners at the university who are underprepared for the rigors of university work, particularly with regard to academic literacy. They are developmental immigrant students (DI students), a term coined by Goldschmidt and Ousey to distinguish these English language learners from other learners. As a result of the difficulties that DI students face with academic literacy and a dearth in the literature that addresses the practical aspects of preparing them for academic literacy, there is a need for a comprehensive pedagogical approach to teaching this population.

For these language learners, learning academic literacy can be a demanding task because they do not necessarily understand what the language of the academy is, which is crucial to college success for them. According to Bartholomae (1985), "Every time a student sits down to write for us, he has to invent the university for the occasion…He has to learn to speak our language, to speak as we do, to try on the peculiar ways of knowing, selecting, evaluating, reporting, concluding, and arguing that define the discourse of our community" (p. 134). In order to help these students understand what academic literacy is, instructors must help students develop their academic literacy and understand its definition.

Traditionally, academic literacy has been defined as "the ability to read and write and compute in the form taught and expected in formal education" (Ogbu, 1995, p. 107). For many years, this particular definition of literacy has been upheld in school curricula, including university courses across the curriculum. Even today, with the influence the No Child Left Behind (NCLB) legislation has had on the PK12 curriculum, academic literacy is still most often defined within this context as nothing more than the ability to read and write. Many researchers (e.g., Cope & Kalantzis, 2000; Lea & Street, 2000) of academic literacy have recognized this definition as being too narrow because it does not include all characteristics of academic literacy. Consequently, the definition has been expanded to include many forms across various domains. Recent research done on academic literacy has extended the definition by examining other characteristics. For example, Scribner and Cole (1981) were the first researchers to introduce the concept of literacy domain to the perspective of literacy. In researching in-school/out-of-school literacy, they realized that there is not just one literacy, but that many forms of it are present in and across different domains of literacy events and practices, which can influence how people learn literacy. Shortly after Scribner and Cole (1981) introduced the concept of literacy domains, Shirley Brice Heath (1983) published her seminal study of the in-school and out-of-school literacy events and practices of children in two small rural towns, Trackton, a primarily African-American community, and Roadville, a primarily white working-class community, located in the Carolinas. What Heath found in looking at the literacy domains of the children in these two small towns was a disconnect between literacy found in one domain compared to literacy found in another: children who were taught school literacy performed better in school than the children who weren't taught the literacy of school. Both of these studies have important implications for the language learning students spotlighted in this book, who generally speak different languages at home and at school; it is only logical that there would be a disconnect in the literacies between the domains of home and school. School literacy must therefore be highlighted and emphasized to these students so that they see and understand the differences.

Other research done on academic literacy found that academic literacies are impacted by context. For example, in most university courses, writing is the means by which students demonstrate their understanding of course material (see Leki, 2007). However, upon closer look, one will see that the required writing genres differ from course to course. Students may be asked to write a critical review essay in their composition course and a lab report in their chemistry course. Students need to understand the different writing conventions and requirements across the curriculum.

Literacy practices, a term coined by the New Literacy Studies group, are the social practices that students would carry out in a university course, such as to write a research paper on an assigned topic, to do the research that's involved in writing this paper, to schedule an individual consultation with the teacher on the writing of it, and possibly to meet with tutors in the writing center to get help with improving the paper. By carrying out the literacy practices that accompany writing a research paper, students are taking part in the social practices that are common at the university (see Swales, 1990). Students, especially DI students who may not have received this information in previous schooling, must be explicitly taught how to succeed in each step; instructors shouldn't assume that they already know what to do to succeed. In addition, students need to understand how to use the various literacies in different university courses, such as written and oral literacy and print and screen-based literacy. Just as Heath (1983) found multiliteracies to be the disconnect between out-of-school literacy and in-school literacy, Ong (1982) found that the distinction between oral and writing cultures is that students must change the way they think, when shifting between the oral and written cultures. Students from an oral culture process and memorize bits of spoken and otherwise irretrievable information quickly, whereas students from a written culture have a text to refer to when conveying information between the originator of a thought and the receiver of it. The majority of DI students are more comfortable with using English orally. Print and screen-based literacy is particularly important for language learning students in terms of their being able to critically evaluate the sources of information found on computers: They need to know that not all information is equal.

Teaching Developmental Immigrant Students in Undergraduate Programs: A Practical Guide by Myra Goldschmidt and Debbie Ousey focuses explicitly and extensively on a wide range of pedagogical approaches to working with developmental immigrant students, which has been greatly needed in the field for some time now. Goldschmidt and Ousey evenhandedly present a definition of Generation 1.5 learners in tandem with a term that designates a sub-group of learners within this group. Over time, defining these particular learners has arguably been one of the most challenging aspects of discussing this group, has long attracted attention in the field, and has provoked debate. However, Goldschmidt and Ousey do a thorough job of clearly identifying this new group of learners.

Goldschmidt and Ousey's discussion of the practical aspect of teaching academic literacy to developmental immigrant students covers a range of topics that impressively extends from fundamental issues, such as the nuts and bolts of creating courses for developmental immigrant students, to more complex issues, such as approaches to teaching academic literacy, including teaching study skills, teaching academic integrity, and teaching a content-based course. Obviously, however, in the nine chapters of this book, Goldschmidt and Ousey do not attempt to provide an exhaustive coverage of any of the topics regarding approaches to teaching developmental immigrant students. Instead, what they do is present the most prevalent academic literacy issues that, from working with these students, they've observed most DI students struggle with. As TESOL pedagogues who have extensive experience working with developmental immigrant students, Goldschmidt and Ousey offer the readers of this book a comprehensive pedagogical approach to the teaching of academic literacy to immigrant students in higher education. The book is a goal-oriented, theoretically based, hands-on resource book. Moreover, it is a "how-to" book that addresses both the academic challenges underprepared students encounter and their need to be connected to a campus community. Finally, it is a "how to" book that approaches this population from a cross-disciplinary perspective, from an ESL and developmental perspective, and from a practical content-driven perspective. Readers of the book who work with this population of learners will be inspired by the ideas contained within the book and be motivated to incorporate, modify, and expand upon them in their classrooms.

——————————————— References

Bartholomae, D. (1985). Inventing the university. In M. Rose (Ed.), *When a writer can't write* (pp. 134-165). New York: The Guilford Press.

Heath, S.B. (1983). *Ways with words: Language, life and work in communities and classrooms*. Cambridge, U.K.: Cambridge University Press.

Leki, I. (2007). *Undergraduates in a second language: Challenges and complexities of academic literacy development*. Mahwah, NJ: Lawrence Erlbaum.

Ogbu, J. (1995). Cultural mode, identity and literacy. In B. Street & J. Street (Eds.). *Social literacies: Critical approaches to literary in development, ethnography, and education*. New York: Longman.

Ong, W. (1982). *Orality and literacy: The technologizing of the word*. London: Metheun.

Scribner, S., & Cole, M. (1981). *The psychology of literacy*. Cambridge, MA: Harvard University Press.

Swales, J. (1990). *Genre analysis: English in academic and research settings*. Cambridge, U.K.: Cambridge University Press.

Acknowledgments

This book is dedicated to teachers: our former teachers, who instilled in us the foundational knowledge for teaching developmental immigrant students; current teachers of developmental immigrant students, who enable these students to thrive in undergraduate programs today; and future teachers of DI students, who will take on the challenge of working with this very special population of students. This book is also about the developmental immigrant students themselves, who have inspired us to write this book and to become better teachers.

Myra and Debbie

One of the rewards of completing a book is the opportunity to thank those individuals who contributed to both the process and the product. We want to thank Cate Crosby, a colleague who continually inspires us with her knowledge, her professionalism, and her enthusiasm; it is truly an honor to work with Cate. Not only did her feedback help us to strengthen the book, but also, by writing the foreword for this book on academic literacy, her area of expertise, she provided the foundation upon which this book is based.

Two faculty members at Penn State Brandywine also deserve recognition: Norma Notzold, for being the quintessential teacher of developmental immigrant students and who, almost single-handedly, has enabled many of our students to succeed because of her dedication and commitment to them; and Christine Flurie Brown, a Penn State Brandywine reading instructor and writing tutor and now the coordinator of our campus learning center, who builds such strong relationships with our developmental immigrant students and is so gifted in both challenging and supporting them. Her insightful and tireless input into both the Reading and Learning Center chapters, along with her feedback on other chapters, tremendously strengthened the book.

Certainly, this book would not have been possible without the support, insight, and expert advice of Kelly Sippell, our editor at the University of Michigan Press. Kelly helped guide this book to completion with a combination of personal warmth and professional expertise, and for that we will always be grateful.

Myra

First and foremost, I want to thank my colleague, Debbie Ousey, for writing this book with me and for her conscientious and thoughtful collaboration throughout the process. Debbie is not only a superb teacher, but she is also a superb individual.

I want to express gratitude to my family: to my husband, Michael, whose unwavering love and support made this book happen; and to my children, Kyle, Claire, Marcela, and Jeremy, for understanding my temporary departure from 'motherhood' during the writing process. Marcela Velez and Jeremy Lawrence deserve a special debt of gratitude, as each provided me with invaluable computer assistance. THANK YOU! Finally, I owe deep appreciation to both my mother, Ruth Straus, who encouraged me to follow in her footsteps and become a teacher, and to my mother-in-law, Ilse Goldschmidt, who taught me the true meaning of perseverance and courage.

Debbie

I first want to thank Myra: her drive, dedication, thoughtfulness, and clear love of her students made this dream of a book a reality and working with her a pleasure.

I dedicate this book to so many: my dear husband, Dave Ousey, and children, Nathan and Teresa, for their patience, love, and support as I tried to fit writing a book into our lives; my parents, Pat and Bill Lamb and siblings (Marty, Colleen, Katie) for their belief and support; Matthew and Betsy Lamb, for entertaining their cousins so beautifully as I worked (and Mary, for providing them!); Terry Keane and Cheri Micheau, forever my models of good teaching, and Dennis Godfrey, whose insightful observations guide my teaching still; and my grandfather, William C. Lamb, Sr., who always saw me as a writer.

I especially thank Harrington "Kit" Crissy for welcoming me so warmly at a PennTESOL-East meeting years ago and thus beginning many happy years of working, teaching, and learning on its board. Jane Gee, Stephanie Zangwill, Linda Fellag, Roger Gee, Sherry Eichert, Linn Lisher: I thank you and so many others in PTE whose support, friendship, encouragement, dedication, and expertise helped me grow as a teacher. Teaching can be isolating work, and PTE strengthened my belief in the importance of encouraging and supporting communities of teachers.

Finally, and most important, I thank my students, past, present, and future, who teach, inspire, and sustain me every day.

Grateful acknowledgment is made to the following authors and publishers for permission to reprint previously published or copyrighted material.

Cate Crosby for Figure 7.2.

Kate Kinsella for material in Figure 9.1.

Norma Notzold for Figure 4.1 and material in Appendix 4b.

Pearson for material from pages I-8 and I-9 of *Writing Talk, Instructor's Edition* by Anthony Winkler and Jo-Ray McCuen-Wetherell. Copyright 2003. Reprinted by permission.

Jennifer Peters for material in Figure 9.2.

Z. Zhang for material in Figure 7.1.

Contents

Introduction

More and more students are entering college in the United States without the academic literacy skills needed to successfully complete their college education. In 2007–2008, approximately one-third of all first-year college students were required to enroll in remedial or developmental courses in four-year institutions (Bettinger & Long, 2009), and 41 percent in two-year institutions (Sladky, 2010), despite the fact that four out of five remedial students had a high school GPA of 3.0 or higher (Sladky, 2010). (Even more alarming are the findings of The American Association of College and Universities [AAC&U] who report that 53 percent of first-year college students are academically underprepared, i.e., lacking basic skills in reading, writing, and/or mathematics [Tritelli, 2003]). Though these staggering percentages represent a diverse group of students with a wide array of abilities, educational backgrounds, family income, and life experiences (Dzubak, 2007), the fact remains that an increasing number of students are underprepared for college and therefore are at-risk for failure as college students.

According to King (2004) "at-risk" students in college include those students who are academically underprepared because of educational risk factors, including academic failure, poor preparation, and low expectations; familial risk factors, including values concerning education and lack of financial resources; and social risk factors, including conflicting ethnic or cultural values or stressful peer and social interactions. Keeling (2003) adds one additional risk factor to King's list: at-risk students enter college lacking educational planning skills or the know-how and steps it takes to earn a college degree. In order to address the many needs of these at-risk students, institutions of higher learning throughout the United States have increasingly been implementing remedial or developmental programs, focusing on reading, writing, and mathematics (Bettinger & Long, 2009). However, for some of these at-risk students, also called developmental students, even the developmental courses are not enough to keep students in college.

One particular group of at-risk developmental students entering both two- and four-year undergraduate programs in large numbers and, unfortunately, dropping out or failing out in large numbers as well, are immigrant students, who tend to need more than one or two remedial courses to be successful in their quest for higher education, despite the fact that they have graduated from U.S. high schools. Developmental immigrant students are a growing phenomenon in the United States, a growing population in higher education, and a growing presence in undergraduate classes, and like their mainstream developmental counterparts, they are academically underprepared for the rigors of college. However, unlike their mainstream developmental counterparts, their linguistic cleavages, especially in writing, and the discrepancies between their expectations and the reality of the college experience and beyond, have created major obstacles to their obtaining academic success.

Furthermore, because this particular population of students, whom we refer to as developmental immigrant students (DI students), has not been the focus of remediation research in higher education, they are usually placed into mainstream classes or developmental classes or ESL classes, which treat these students as *only* mainstream, or *only* developmental or *only* ESL learners, depending on the specialized training of the instructor. The reality for most DI students, however, is that they are all three types: they are developmental students, from (mostly) non-English speaking backgrounds, who have, for the most part, been in mainstream classes in the United States. The reality for college instructors is that this population of students needs to be discussed because their growing numbers indicate that a discussion is warranted: English language learners, including DI students, will comprise approximately 65 percent of the U.S. population growth through the year 2020 (Spanier, 2004).

Our rationale for writing the book is four-fold. First, we wanted to respond to the need for a comprehensive approach in teaching DI students in undergraduate programs. Up until now, most of the literature on teaching English language learners has focused on traditional ESL students or on Generation 1.5 students, paying particular attention to challenges with writing and reading. This book provides a comprehensive framework for DI students, focusing on multiple academic literacy challenges, to help them overcome the obstacles they encounter in college.

The second reason for writing this book is that even though many students coming to our campus (Penn State Brandywine) are underprepared for the rigors of college, DI students, in particular, seem to be less prepared for college than many students as few of their academic literacy skills are well developed for higher education (Allison, 2009). One reason for this underpreparedness is that DI students are still developing their cognitive academic language proficiency: it usually takes 5–7 years to develop CALP (Cummins, 1979). In addition, it seems that the increased standardized testing in public schools has changed the nature of the classroom, encouraging fewer critical thinking tasks (mostly true-false, multiple choice, matching, and sentence completion worksheets and tests); less connected and cohesive reading assignments; and little academic Internet use (Allison, 2009). The extent to which DI students can manipulate and navigate literacy greatly impacts how successful their post secondary academic efforts will be (Hirvela, 2004).

The third reason for writing this book is to fill a void: teachers who have these at-risk DI students in their classes are not sure how to teach them, and most of the textbooks on immigrant students focus only on writing or only on reading or are edited collections of essays or case studies. None focus on the comprehensive needs of these students. Tinto (2004), Boylan (2001), and McGillin (2003) have shown that the success rate for academically underprepared students, including DI students, can increase by offering a developmental program that provides effective advising (a key component for academic, social and personal success); content and structure (pre-college basic skills courses, tutoring, and topical workshops); and instructors and tutors who believe that students can succeed, despite the sometimes improbable circumstances. We have created such a program, and most of our DI students have become successful college students.

Finally, the fourth reason for writing this book is to share our joy in teaching DI students: we have derived so much pleasure in watching the students grow, both bilingually and bi-culturally, that we wanted to share our lessons, both literally and figuratively, with those faculty who are, or who will be, fortunate enough to teach them. In fact, our students' (unedited) voices are *heard* throughout the book to remind us never to lose sight of why we are teaching them.

This book is divided into three parts, and each chapter begins with the key points highlighted in the chapter. Part I, Developmental Immigrant Students and Academic Literacy (Chapters 1–2), details the challenges faced by DI students and the faculty that teach them and describes some programming options. Part II, Partnering with Campus Support Programs (Chapters 3–4), discusses using a collaborative approach, partnering with learning and writing centers, and/or advising staff and appropriate administrators, in order to maximize DI student benefits in higher education. Part III, Teaching Literacy within an Academic Framework: Suggested Approaches (Chapters 5–9), provides specific approaches that we have found particularly beneficial in teaching DI students. Each chapter identifies specific goals to address problematic issues for the DI students (issues that were not being met in just mainstream, developmental, or ESL courses). The suggested approaches to meet each goal are intentionally specific to provide teachers across the disciplines with concrete activities and methods that can be implemented and built upon in their own classrooms. It is our hope that instructors who have DI students in their classes use these goals and approaches as a menu of ideas to help meet their students' needs, to create their own materials, and to add to their teaching repertoire. The book concludes with several appendixes containing additional classroom resources.

Thus, we offer this resource book to all of the stakeholders involved in the undergraduate education of DI students.

Part I

Developmental Immigrant Students and Academic Literacy

Chapter 1

Who Are Developmental Immigrant Students?

KEY POINTS

☞ Developmental immigrant students are entering undergraduate programs throughout the United States with the same hopes and dreams as most college students: to graduate, to find a good job, and to become successful citizens.

☞ Teachers have the opportunity and privilege to help these students reach their academic goals.

When I came to the country, I always thought that this country was 'the land of opportunity' or 'the promised land.' In order for me to be free, I have to cross over the gate [education], which I have not yet crossed over.

—first-year developmental immigrant student

Before we can define developmental immigrant (DI) students, it is important to distinguish these students from other first-year college students. Certainly, the majority of students entering colleges and universities in the United States are ready to do so: two-thirds of all students complete their education with varying degrees of success. It is the other one-third of first-year students who are academically underprepared and, therefore, more likely to drop out of college (Sladky, 2010). Often, these students are placed into remedial courses, but encounter difficulties in completing these courses and, ultimately, their college education. However, it is also true that every year more than half a million academically underprepared college students do successfully complete their remedial courses, precisely because of the developmental approach when working with these students (Boylan, 2001), and go on to do as well in standard classes as those students who began their education fully prepared (McCabe, 2000).

In this book, we will address the underprepared "third" of entering college students (using the more optimistic statistic of the two cited in the introduction), who have traditionally been categorized as either developmental students or ESL students and placed into either mainstream developmental classes or ESL classes in the first year of college (and sometimes beyond). Certainly, many of these students are, in fact, (mainstream) developmental students or ESL students and belong in these classes. However, in the last twenty years, a new cohort of students, Generation 1.5, has emerged on college campuses across the nation, and for two decades, researchers and teachers have been defining and describing these students: some of them have been found to struggle in the mainstream developmental and ESL classes because they fall somewhere between the two groups (Roberge, 2003; Harklau, 2000). We too have researched and taught Generation 1.5 students at our campus, Penn State Brandywine (a Pennsylvania State University campus in the Philadelphia area). Originally, these students were also placed into ESL composition classes, but we soon realized that one or two composition classes were not enough to retain them; they could not cope in their General Education classes, so most dropped out or failed out of college. We also realized that within the Generation 1.5 cohort, there was a sub-group of learners, whom we have labeled developmental immigrant students (DI students), who seemed to need even more comprehensive and intrusive developmental work if they were to succeed in college.

The following section begins with a brief comment about our challenges in labeling DI students (let alone any group of students), and will be followed by definitions of ESL students, Generation 1.5 students, traditional developmental students (non-ESL), and DI students.

Labels in general are problematic because they are fraught with problems and dilemmas of their own; they stigmatize and marginalize, but labels have always been used as a tool for identification in education, especially in identifying students, because they help to provide a frame of reference. Therefore, we have identified (and labeled) a sub-group of Generation 1.5 students flooding college campuses today as developmental immigrant (DI) students.

Following are definitions of those students that have been identified, for the most part, as students needing remedial or developmental course work on many college campuses: mainstream developmental students, ESL students, Generation 1.5, and DI students.

Mainstream Developmental Students

Developmental (remedial) education is a result of Open Admissions policies that began in the 1970s: students were suddenly being admitted into institutions of higher learning unprepared for the rigors of college, thus needing remedial support. Developmental programs in higher education approach students and their learning holistically: they are based on the belief that all learners possess innate abilities, which can be used to support growth in lesser developed areas (Mulvey, 2008). Rather than focusing solely on weak skill areas, a developmental approach assumes that everyone has talents and strengths. By acknowledging these strengths while building those areas that are underdeveloped, faculty encourage students to become more competent and confident learners (Casazza, 1999).

Actually, a positive approach is what has enabled so many "at risk" students to realize their dream of a college degree since 1869, when Charles W. Eliot, the president of Harvard at the time, stated that "The American college is obliged to supplement the American school. Whatever elementary instruction the schools fail to give, the college must supply" (Spann, 2000, p. 2). Eliot's words express the true American ideal of equality for all: we have a moral obligation to try to level the playing field when there is a way to do so. In other words, developmental education is about increasing students' chances for success in order to "increase their social and economic well being, which, in turn, will increase the social and economic well being of our country" (Spann, 2000, p. 2). Spann, who authored the Education Commission of the United States' Policy on post-secondary remediation, found that developmental education, combined with quality learning support systems—tutoring, counseling, etc.—can translate into long-term success for students.

ESL Students

Through the years, the label English as a second language (ESL) has referred to any student whose native language is a language other than English; however, this term has always been problematic since, in many cases, English is not necessarily the second language of these students, but rather the third or fourth language. For this reason, other terms have been used to identify these students: language minority student, limited English–proficient student (LEP), English language learner (ELL), and so forth. However, regardless of the acronym used and regardless of the nuances that may distinguish one acronym from another in colleges and universities, most instructors at least have a sense that the student in question is an ESL student; they have a frame of reference that the student is a non-native English speaker.

For the most part, ESL students are more proficient in written English than in spoken English as many learned (formal) written English in language classes in their native countries; they are literate in their first language (they have usually had uninterrupted spoken and written L1 development); they have a meta-language for discussing aspects of language learning because of their background in L1 academic literacy; and they have little understanding of U.S. culture or its educational systems since most completed their PK–12 education in their home countries. Many ESL students are placed into ESL composition classes or into mainstream developmental classes in their first year of college.

Generation 1.5 Students

When a relatively new population of immigrant students who seemed to embody different characteristics from the ESL students began entering U.S. colleges and universities in the last twenty years, a new term was coined to label them, Generation 1.5 (Rumbaut & Ima, 1988). And as these students began to be studied, the label seemed appropriate; it was a category that distinguished them from ESL students. However, the more that has been learned about Generation 1.5, the more the label is being questioned. (The term was coined as a sociological term, not a linguistic one, so it didn't take into consideration linguistic variation.) With that said, the term Generation 1.5 is still recognized by faculty in colleges and universities throughout the United States, and it is also still used in some journal articles and books, although much less so now.

Much has been written about Generation 1.5, and much has been learned about this population in the last twenty years. They come from non–English speaking backgrounds and have "traits and experiences [that] lie somewhere between those associated with the first and second generation" (Rumbaut & Ima, 1988, p. 103). They are U.S. residents through naturalization, green card, or birth; tend to "live" their native culture at home and their adopted culture at school; and are usually the first generation in their families to attend university in the United States.

It has been well documented (Harklau, Losey, & Siegal, 1999; Roberge, 2003; Goldschmidt & Ziemba, 2003) that the education Generation 1.5 students receive prior to attending post-secondary institutions varies tremendously, so they usually enter higher education with diverse educational experiences, diverse English language proficiencies, and diverse academic literacies (Patton, 2006). For those Generation 1.5 students born outside of the United States, they have come to the U.S. either voluntarily or involuntarily; they may or may not have had an interrupted first language (L1) development; and they may have a presence or absence of L1 literacy and/or other language literacy (Harklau et al., 1999; Leki, 1992; Ogbu, 1991; Roberge, 2002; Rumbaut & Ima, 1988). Thus, they graduate from U.S. high schools with varying degrees of education and with "varying degrees of bilingualism, biculturalism, and academic literacy" (Danico, 2004; Skarin, 2001; Harklau, Losey, & Siegal, 1999).

Because most of these students come to the United States at some point during their schooling period, they are at least partially U.S. educated; therefore, many do not identify themselves as English language learners nor do they fully recognize their problems with reading and writing because their oral fluency is usually strong. In high school these students are well behaved and conscientious, but the academic demands placed on them are often not sufficient for the rigors of college.

At Penn State Brandywine, most of our non-native English-speaking students embody the characteristics of Generation 1.5; however, in the last five years (since 2005) they have been more underprepared and more in need of support, both in and out of the classroom, than in previous years. Though they are English dominant at this point in their education, in reality they have a very limited formal knowledge of English (Hedgcock & Ferris, 2009); therefore, we have identified these most at-risk students within Generation 1.5 as developmental immigrant students.

Developmental Immigrant Students

Though DI students share many of the same characteristics as Generation 1.5, they tend to face greater academic, social, and emotional challenges in their pursuit of higher education. Also, because DI students have not been specifically described in the literature, we wanted to shed greater light on them to fill a gaping hole in the ongoing discussion on Generation 1.5: it is not our intention to separate developmental immigrant students from Generation 1.5 but rather to include this group in the dialogue as a subset of Generation 1.5. We coined the term *developmental immigrant student* because this student is a first or second generation immigrant student who needs (extensive) developmental course work.

Usually, when DI students enter post-secondary education, they are placed into one of two (usually non-credit) English classes: an ESL class, where many of the students can read and write English but have trouble speaking English, or a developmental class, which is mostly comprised of traditional students (who lack academic literacy skills) and which is usually taught by an instructor who does not have an ESL background. Developmental immigrant students' needs fall somewhere in between: They tend to have weak reading and writing English skills but strong oral skills, and they need developmental and academic literacy skills (taught by a teacher with an ESL background) to be able to compete at the college level. In other words, within the broad spectrum of Generation 1.5, developmental immigrant students tend to have the greatest number of challenges and the least amount of self-sufficiency. In addition to literacy issues, these students often have to support themselves and/or finance their own education, sometimes have few family members to turn to in the United States, and usually have no frame of reference for the system of U.S. higher education.

It is important to understand that developmental placement, especially in the first year, is not unusual in undergraduate programs. As stated in the introduction, about one-third of freshmen in four-year colleges (Bettinger & Long, 2009) and universities and 41 percent of freshmen in community colleges in 2007–2008 required remedial education (Sladky, 2010), despite the fact that 4 out of 5 developmental or remedial students graduated from high school with a GPA of 3.0 or higher. For immigrant students, especially, being placed into developmental classes often confuses them: they don't understand the ramifications of what they did or did not receive academically until they transition into college. In college, they begin their process into becoming "educated" people (Levinson & Holland, 1996), a process which usually clarifies, sometimes painfully so, the extent of their preparedness, or lack thereof, from their previous academic training. Roberge (2003) puts it bluntly when he says that this lack of preparedness is often the result of their pre–college based acquisition processes, where they experience a merry-go-round of placements, pedagogies, and teaching practices resulting in inconsistent instruction. Thus, it is the student who needs a solid academic literacy foundation, along with a strong system of academic support, that we refer to as a developmental immigrant student.

A few years ago, a student was admitted to our campus because of her impressive high school GPA (3.7). She had come to the United States at the age of 16, was placed in the 11th grade in high school, and graduated near the top of her class. However, her admission to university brought with it new challenges and realities. The student's combined SAT score was 400 (200 Verbal; 200 Math). Also, because she came from a war-torn country, her previous educational experience was sporadic, at best, causing her to have limited foundational knowledge. Much to her amazement and dismay, she was placed in developmental courses at our university, several of which she had to repeat. For this student and others like her, the first year of college turned into a series of frustrations and disappointments. For us, understanding these students' frustrations and disappointments led us to take steps to provide meaningful course work. In fact, this student would come to represent the new immigrant student on our campus.

Perhaps the best way to exemplify DI students is through another student's words sent to his professor in an email a few weeks into the first semester:

I'm total failing in school i'm ready to do for my schoolwork before, but I think I just want to quit my school now i do everything so hard i don't know what can i do? i really want to someone support me. someone help me. but i'm to shy to ask. i don't know i need help.

—first-year developmental immigrant student

While many may see this student as an anomaly, the fact remains that he and thousands of others like him are entering colleges and universities and are struggling to make their way through. But the journey for them is more complex than for most students: This student's words suggest that DI students are not just in need of academic support; they are also in need of emotional and social support. These are students who, despite being admitted into an undergraduate program (again, based primarily on strong high school GPAs), will likely not complete the program without extensive and intrusive support. We believe that DI students' academic literacy needs (along with their emotional and social needs) extend beyond what can realistically be addressed in many undergraduate ESL composition and mainstream developmental classes, yet most undergraduate programs only offer these two options for first-year immigrant students. Table 1.1 provides an overview of the academic literacy practices of developmental L1 students, ESL students, and DI students, framing the similarities and differences among them.

It is important to note that though this chart is used for purposes of comparison/ contrast, there is overlap between categories. However, it is clear that DI students fall somewhere between developmental L1 and ESL students. Like developmental L1 students, DI students need to be taught to distinguish between formal and informal language, need to learn study skills and strategies for reading and writing, and to an even greater extent than developmental L1 students, need to develop academic vocabulary. DI students also need instructors and support staff that understand their needs as students who learned English orally and may have had varied educational experiences. For these students, special attention to grammatical errors (especially word endings and similar-sounding words), idioms and expressions that should and should not be used in academic writing, cultural and historical information about the United States, and academic expectations in higher education are critical to DI students' academic growth.

An overview of some of the challenges facing undergraduate DI students and the faculty who teach them follows. (Please note that in this book, the terms *instructors*, *faculty*, and *professors* are used interchangeably.)

Challenges Faced by DI Students

1. Identity

It has widely been viewed that the college experience offers students opportunities to develop their personal and professional identity (Hamrick, Evans, & Schuh, 2002). Muuss (1996) reinforces this view by saying that the late adolescent years (18–22) are a "crucial time for identity formation" (p. 62) and the overwhelming majority (98 percent) of first-year students fall into this age group (Cooperative Institutional Research Program, 2005). However, it is also true that many of today's first-year college students are more focused on daily life management (Clydesdale, 2007) than they are on identity formation because of family or other circumstances.

Perhaps James M. Lang (2008) puts it best by saying, "It's time to figure out how to work with the freshmen we have, rather than the ones in our admissions brochures"

TABLE 1.1
Academic Literacy Practices of Developmental L1, ESL,
and Developmental Immigrant Students (adapted from Crosby, 2007)

Characteristics	Developmental L1 Students	ESL Students	Developmental Immigrant Students
Language Proficiency	Speak and write English as an L1	Speak and write another language as an L1, also possibly speak other languages, also possibly write other languages	May speak another language as an L1 (sometimes limited or not at all), also possibly speak other languages (not necessarily fluently), sometimes write another language as an L1, also possibly write other languages
L1 Proficiency	Uninterrupted spoken and written L1 development	Uninterrupted spoken and written L1 development	Sometimes interrupted or no written L1 development; sometimes interrupted spoken L1 development
English Language Learning	Acquired spoken and written English	Learned mostly written English in formal language classes	Learned mostly spoken English by exposure to it
English Proficiency	Tend to use only informal English in speaking and writing	More proficient in written English than spoken English; more familiar with formal than informal English	More proficient in informal spoken English (BICS — Basic Interpersonal Communicative Skills) (Cummins, 1981) than formal written English; more familiar with other varieties of English than standard American English
Educational Background	Complete PK12 schooling in U.S.	Complete PK12 schooling in home country	Usually complete part of PK12 schooling in home country; complete other part of PK12 schooling in U.S.
Understanding of U.S. Culture	Understanding of U.S. culture, educational school systems	Little understanding of U.S. culture, educational school systems	Some understanding of U.S. culture, educational school systems
Academic Literacies Proficiency	Weak background in academic literacies in English	Background in academic literacies in L1; some to no background in academic literacies in English	Some background in academic literacies in English; some to no background in academic literacies in L1
BICS and CALP Proficiency (Cummins, 1997)	Strong BICS, developing CALP (Cognitive Academic Language Proficiency) (Cummins, 1981)—academic English learner	Developing BICS and CALP — learning academic as well as other types of English	Strong BICS, developing CALP — academic English learner (further behind developmental L1 learners)
Difficulties with Academic Literacies	Difficulties with fluency in academic writing from lack of academic writing experience, difficulties with comprehending academic readings from lack of practice and exposure	Difficulties with fluency in academic writing, interference from L1, misuse and misunderstanding of idiomatic expressions, difficulties with comprehending academic readings from lack of practice and exposure	Difficulties with fluency in academic writing, phonetic quality to writing — inclusion of idiomatic and non-standard English expressions, difficulties with comprehending academic readings from lack of practice and exposure
Meta-Language Proficiency	Meta-language for discussing language, but only if learners had foreign language learning experience	Meta-language for discussing aspects of language learning	Very little or no meta-language for discussing aspects of language learning
Grammatical Proficiency	Grammatical errors include subject-verb agreement, noun/pronoun-reference, possessive form	Grammatical errors include subject-verb agreement, noun-pronouns, articles, prepositions, verb tense	Grammatical errors include verb endings, noun endings, verb tense, subject-verb agreement, articles, prepositions

(C1, *Chronicle of Higher Education*). Lang clarifies this statement by explaining that first-year students spend most of their time and intellectual energy figuring out how to handle life: dealing with money, negotiating newfound freedoms with sex, drugs, and alcohol, and determining how much time to devote to studying, working, and playing, rather than figuring out who they are, as they actively resist efforts "to examine their self-understandings through classes or to engage their humanity through institutional efforts such as public lectures, the arts, or social activism" (C1).

The college experience is a crucial time for both identity formation and time management, but it is also a time of role confusion (Erikson, 1950). Because college-aged DI students share cultural characteristics of both the first and second generation, they are even more confused in some ways, continually reassessing who they are in relation to their families and friends and school; sometimes they are just not sure who they are. Their life experiences are such that they experience dual cultures, languages, traditions, and identifications, fluctuating back and forth between them. This experience exacerbates college confusion because they are not only learning about the culture of higher education, they are also learning about their own culture and identity within the wider culture. For the most part, these students stop learning about native cultural knowledge when they leave their native lands, knowledge that is critical in identity formation. No matter when the students leave their native country, identity formation is in various stages of completeness. If students are born in the United States, in contrast, native identity formation is more often gleaned rather than actively learned or experienced. Also, depending on when DI students arrive in this country, their education begins at the same point as their classmates in terms of age, but not at the same point as their classmates in terms of academic literacy.

2. Language and Background Knowledge

Language-wise, many DI students' first language development was "interrupted," so they tend to be somewhere between the learning of one language and the learning of another as well as somewhere between their acquired (mostly spoken) English and their academic (mostly written) English. Also, because most of them are ear learners, learning English through listening (Reid, 1997), they usually speak English fluently, often as fluently as native speakers because of their strong social skills (Harklau, 2003).

Though English skills continually improve in college, DI students still tend to lag behind native speakers in reading and writing: their reading and writing is usually English-dominant, but they lack a basis of comparison in a fully developed L1 language system (Thonus, 2003). In addition, although some have read novels in high school (remarkably, some have not), they are not necessarily familiar with the content-specific language of academic texts.

Finally, many DI students lack background knowledge in the content subjects they are studying and therefore struggle in these classes, especially in comprehending lectures and taking notes (Kiang, 1992) and reading and studying from textbooks (Spack, 1997). This struggle further exacerbates their frustration as they pursue higher education.

3. Navigating Higher Education

The fact that DI students graduated from U.S. high schools and are somewhat familiar with contemporary American culture is deceiving because they are often challenged by the American higher education system (Harklau, Losey, & Siegal, 1999; Harklau, 2000). In this respect, DI students are usually caught between expectations and reality in their undergraduate education.

The problem usually begins at the pre–college level where DI students may be placed in classes that are academically and socially "discontinuous with the norms for literate expression they encounter upon entering college" (Oakes, Gamoran, & Page 1992), perilously decreasing their chances of success in college. In these basic classes, students have little contact with academic texts, limiting their experience with academic reading and writing, but they tend to do well and get high grades because they show up and work hard. Despite the good grades and hard work, however, most are placed into developmental classes when they enter college, placement that causes them much anger and frustration. In college, this frustration is usually grounded in the fact that developmental classes put them behind where they think that they should be, making their education more expensive and taking much longer since many of these classes don't count for college credit.

What further complicates the problem for them is that they hold a U.S. high school diploma. Administrators and faculty *expect* these students to do well precisely because they have graduated from U.S. high schools and because they often show evidence of stereotypes (committed, hard working, serious) associated with international students (Harklau, 1998). Likewise, these students *expect* to do well because they have gone through (at least in part) the U.S. school system and have graduated, usually with a high grade point average, from this system. The discrepancy in expectations is largely responsible for the confusion, frustration, and, sometimes, failure that developmental immigrant students face in higher education.

Another complication for the students is that they and their families sometimes have misconceived notions of what attending college means. For parents who have never attended college, especially college in the United States, there are few expectations of college other than that their children will get a good education to ensure that they have a good life. Neither parents nor students have a realistic frame of reference regarding the rigorous commitment required in higher education. Also, many parents do not see a problem with their children working full time (40+ hours a week) or with taking care of siblings full time while going to school. Some of these parents are, themselves, working long hours in low-paying jobs in their quest to survive and to provide for their families. It is not unusual for students to help the family at work or at home, perilously overloading an already full academic schedule.

Like their parents, DI students are not sure what to expect from higher education. Most see college as an extension of high school. They know that they have to work hard, and they equate hard work with success, which, at this level and for this population, may not be enough.

The expectations by teachers and administrators about immigrant students can also be incongruent with the expectations by these students and their families about the U.S. educational system. Students who enter university lacking what Bourdieu (1998) refers to as "academic culture capital," the processes or the valued practices of education (those practices and activities that are part of higher education, such as advocating for oneself, understanding the language and vocabulary, etc.), will usually have difficulty identifying and interpreting these practices and the expectations inherent within them, thus diminishing their chances of completing higher education. Ironically, the educational opportunity available to these students is precisely the reason why many of them came to the United States in the first place, equating success with a college degree.

This lack of academic culture capital among students creates tremendous gaps in understanding (Harklau, 1998) between college educators and the students themselves concerning the academic preparedness of these students. Because these gaps are usually at the subconscious level on the part of students and teachers, neither group recognizes them as a problem. Zamel (1991) explains that "not only do students need to learn how language form and language function are interrelated, how discourse and context are interdependent, and how language and culture are intertwined, but ESL students [as well as DI students] also need to learn how higher education operates in terms of its expectations, assumptions, and conventions."

Challenges Faced by Faculty of DI Students

One of the greatest challenges faced by faculty in undergraduate programs is what to do with underprepared students sitting in their classes: these are the students that are struggling to stay in school; these are the one-third of first-year students that will fail or quit one or more of their classes (Chute, 2008). And certainly, some of these students are DI students who face even more obstacles because of language and literacy.

Some faculty may question how these DI students (as well as mainstream developmental students) get admitted to college (usually because of strong high school GPAs) considering their underpreparedness, but the fact remains that they are in our colleges and universities. Though college admission processes are outside the scope of this book, the questions that faculty really need to ask is how can they best serve these students that have been admitted, and how can they give them the opportunity to thrive. At the very least, instructors in undergraduate programs should assess the immigrant students sitting in their classrooms and respond to them accordingly: understanding who these students are and how they learn, which, ultimately, will help in answering how they can best be served.

Complicating the problem of how to best serve DI students is the fact that less than 13 percent of teachers have had any professional development on teaching any English language learners (NCTE, 2008), let alone those most at-risk. Many instructors honestly don't know what to do with students with relatively undeveloped language and literacy skills (Hedgcock & Ferris, 2009). Certainly a strong support system helps (learning center, writing center, etc.), but is that enough to ensure student success?

Following are some of the challenges that faculty face in the classroom, challenges that, in some ways, are mirrored by the students' own challenges.

1. Student Underpreparedness

What surprises some instructors are the writing errors: DI students speak well and "sound" American; therefore, the assumption is that they can write well in English too. The underlying assumption here is that the students' spoken English proficiency equals that of their written proficiency. Thus, DI students may be in classes for weeks before instructors notice problems (e.g., when the first big paper is due); therefore, it might be helpful for instructors to give students a writing assignment early in the semester to try to identify those students needing extra writing support.

Perhaps the most problematic issue is a tendency by some faculty to look at immigrant students through a deficit lens (Davies, Safarik, & Banning, 2003), seeing weak writing skills or a lack of preparedness rather than the rich diversity they bring to the classroom and college or university. Roberge (2003) reinforces this by stating that when teachers compare English language learners with monolingual learners, they tend to focus on deficiencies rather than strengths.

Adding to the problem of student underpreparedness is the fact that some faculty are not sure how to teach them other than to "apply monolingual standards to immigrants' bilingual performance" (Ward, 1997, B8). Students for whom English is not the native language should not necessarily be held to the same standards, especially in writing, as students whose only language is English.

2. Non-Academic Issues of DI Students

Faculty should be sensitive to the many non-academic issues that DI students bring to college with them. As with mainstream students, many of them have demanding home or family responsibilities, grinding job commitments, and/or troubling financial burdens, but DI students are often the translator for the entire family, which means going to medical appointments with all family members, dealing with younger siblings' school forms, and reading all sorts of bills and/or government forms. Many DI students are also the (primary) caregivers to younger siblings in the family and some are responsible for providing food and clothing for them. Most of the students are too embarrassed to tell instructors about any problems they may have, problems that are not academic ones, but which are enough to cause them to drop out of college.

3. Instructors Unfamiliar with and Untrained in Teaching DI Students

Some instructors lack an understanding of the students' differing expectations of schooling, their differing reading and writing experiences, and their differing learning styles: all of these impact the students' classroom learning experience. Specifically, some instructors are unfamiliar with how DI students process a language, how they learn a language, and how they are motivated to learn. For the most part, they learn differently from the way that most American students have been taught in that they haven't done much reading in English. Also, because many DI students have had various sources of academic input throughout their schooling years, there are gaps in academic development. Some students attended school in their native country while others did not; some have been taught by ESL teachers and some by non-ESL teachers; and some have attended a variety of schools in different states or countries. Finally, because of their varied learning experiences, DI students are unfamiliar with differences in language use: formal (written) language vs. informal (spoken) language, a fact that many college faculty are not aware of. Instructors need to know what on-campus support exists and/or where to refer DI students should problems arise.

4. Student Advising and Placement

Finally, in their role as academic advisors, discipline instructors should be aware of DI students' reading and writing proficiency levels, information that is usually found in the admissions office. Sometimes, based solely on the students' high school grades or the strength of their oral proficiency, faculty place them into courses that they cannot handle, or they tell the students that they don't need developmental courses because they speak so well. DI students would be better served if faculty had more realistic information about the students' academic literacy skills. Admissions personnel or ESL faculty should be able to provide advisors with this type of information.

The misconceived notions and misinterpretations among DI students are largely responsible for their confusion and frustration in undergraduate programs, and the misunderstandings about these students by faculty are largely responsible for their confusion and frustration regarding these students' ability and performance in the classroom. Though some institutions of higher learning have recognized the special needs of DI students and offer writing programs (Frodesen, 2001; Goen et. al, 2001) or developmental programs (Murie, 2001; Murie & Fitzpatrick, 2009; Goldschmidt & Ziemba, 2003), little research has been done regarding these students' expectations regarding higher education. What is known, however, is that there seems to be a discrepancy in expectations on the part of both the students and the faculty: both expect immigrant students to do well and both are bewildered when they don't.

——— **Chapter 2** ———

Approaches to Teaching Academic Literacy

KEY POINTS

- New courses and programs that address the unique needs of developmental immigrant students are being developed on college campuses throughout the United States.

- Instructors can customize courses and programs on their own campuses by drawing from programs at other campuses.

...I thought it was really hard to understand. The tone and the terms he was using. Like he talked about Karl Marx and how his opinion relates to identity. I'm like okay, he's the person who came up with Communism. That's all I know. Like I understood every single word, but I don't understand what he was talking about. Like I read it and I read it and I'm like Oh my god, I'm dying. But every single word I could understand what he is trying to say.

—first-year developmental immigrant student

In 2000, Penn State Brandywine saw an increase in Generation 1.5 students, and like our previous ESL students, they were placed into an ESL composition class in addition to their general education classes. Soon the Generation 1.5 students were dropping the general education courses (psychology, history, sociology, etc.) during their first semester because they could not keep up with the course requirements. Although the students were receiving extra help in these courses in the learning center, they confessed to the learning center staff that the academic requirements were too overwhelming. Also, the students revealed that they were reluctant to participate in class or speak to an instructor for clarification or for help because of language and cultural barriers. Faculty members, too, expressed their concerns about the *new* ESL students in their classes because they did not appear to be connected in any way to the class or the campus community, and they did not appear to feel confident in making their way through the university system—asking questions, looking for help, or being advocates for themselves within the system.

The reality at our campus and on college campuses throughout the country was that this seemingly new type of ESL student was entering post-secondary institutions in large numbers, bringing new challenges that needed to be addressed. Perhaps nowhere was this reality more evident than at conferences in the fields of TESOL, Linguistics, and Composition where there was a dramatic increase in sessions (usually standing room only) on Generation 1.5 in higher education. These sessions, which mostly addressed the weak academic literacy skills and poor participation among these students, generated a national conversation on educating them or, at the very least, on recognizing that they didn't seem to fit into any of the traditional educational slots: mainstream courses, ESL courses, or mainstream developmental courses. With this recognition came new questions: How do we teach these students who seem to fall somewhere between the traditional ESL student (who primarily needs to acquire *language* for college-level coursework rather than *academic literacy* [Murie & Fitzpatrick, 2009]) and the monolingual developmental student? How do we enable these students to compete with their peers? How do we retain these students so that they can complete their higher education?

Two instructors from the learning center brought these questions to the attention of the ESL professor in the English department, and the three of them determined that Penn State Brandywine needed to create a program for these students so that they could compete in their quest for higher education. In the new millennium, the campus had experienced a rapid increase in Generation 1.5 students, especially those without the basic academic skills needed for college (that we refer to as developmental immigrant students), reflecting an overall increase of Generation 1.5 in K–12 throughout the state and country. In the Commonwealth of Pennsylvania for a ten-year period, the overall K-12 population has decreased by 11.37 percent while the Limited English Proficiency (LEP) population had increased by 57.6 percent. National statistics for the same period showed that the K-12 population had increased 12 percent while the LEP population had increased by 95 percent (National Clearinghouse of English Language Acquisition & Language Instruction Educational Programs, 2003). With statistics like these in hand, along with concerns from campus faculty, and charts of the predicted and actual GPAs of our new immigrant students, the three faculty met with the Dean of Academics. With his permission and the help of a Penn State diversity grant, the instructors began to explore how to create such a program, and they began by looking at the types of courses and programs being offered at other colleges and universities.

Creating Courses and Programs for Generation 1.5

Courses and programs were being created for Generation 1.5 students in institutions of higher learning across the country: some credit-bearing programs and some not, some pre-college admission programs and some post-college admission, some focusing on writing issues and some focusing on developmental issues, some intensive programs and some more 'traditional' college programs. Regardless of the course or program, the dilemma facing undergraduate institutions was how to teach Generation 1.5, including the most underprepared DI students, to become academically literate: teaching them to read, write, and speak the language of the academy, with all the conventions of its discourse (Williams & Snipper, 1990).

An overview of some of the more typical approaches to teaching Generation 1.5 in their first year of college follows.

1. ESL Writing Classes

Many colleges and universities offer ESL writing courses as an alternative to mainstream or developmental first-year writing courses. Placement into ESL writing courses can be somewhat problematic however. Those students who self-identify as ESL students (not too many do) or who are identified by the university or college as non-native speakers of English and who test into a basic level English class on the college entrance exam are usually placed into ESL courses, which are as varied as the instructors who teach them and the departments that house them: ESL, English, Modern Languages, etc.

Williams (1995) found in a survey of universities in the United States that almost every institution that identifies ESL students at admission has some sort of separate ESL course or sequence of courses, and most require that students complete these courses prior to college admission (Harklau et.al., 1999). In institutions where ESL writing courses are offered to matriculated students, the courses may not be credit-bearing or count toward graduation requirements (Williams, 1995).

A program addressing both the writing *and* reading needs of 'at-risk' ESL students is the Developmental Education Program (DEP) at Brooklyn College of the City University of New York. In this program, students learn academic literacy skills by taking control of their reading and writing, connecting their own life experiences to those of academic life, language, and community (Maloney, 2003). Brooklyn College's program has not only enabled students to become better readers, writers, and thinkers, but it has also enabled the students to pass the university-mandated proficiency exam and to graduate from college (Maloney, 2003).

2. Content-Based Instruction: Linking Language Learning with a Content Course

A second approach to teaching L2 students, stemming from the early 1980s, integrates language learning with a content course. There has been much research to support the effective use of content-based learning at the undergraduate level. Mohan (1986) stresses the importance of integrating content and language instruction since most L2 students do not just learn a language, but rather they learn subject matter through the medium of a language. Smoke (1988) reinforces the importance of connecting content with language learning as well, stating that "students need to see that language skills develop within meaningful context and colleges can best provide for ESL students by making this experience available" (p. 17), while Krashen (1981a) says that that connected subject matter promotes language acquisition. Kasper et al. (2000) show that content-based instruction for L2 students not only increases students' English language proficiency, but it also helps them transition well into their mainstream courses and teaches them those skills necessary to be successful in these courses. Blanton (1992) refers to this approach as "holistic" since students become intellectually and cognitively immersed in language and content, much more so than just a skills approach could ever accommodate (Blanton, 1992).

Not only has the research been extensive, but the range of courses that offers content-based instruction has also been extensive: history (Strole, 1997); art history (Raphan & Moser, 1994); literature (Holten, 1997); film (Capple & Curtis, 2000); and mathematics (Cantoni-Harvey, 1987).

A particular type of content-based learning that is offered in many two-year and four-year institutions is called *linked* courses, where a specially designed language course is linked to a content course. In linked courses, students are enrolled in a mainstream content course, but they may not have the necessary academic literacy skills to compete successfully in this course, thus an adjunct course supports the content course. Both courses share the same content; however, the discipline instructor focuses on content while the language instructor focuses on language skills within the context of the discipline (Duenas, 2004). An excellent example of linked course instruction is found in the Introduction of Psychology course, which is part of the Freshman Summer Program at the University of California, Los Angeles. Linked courses can benefit DI students, especially, by pinpointing language issues and offering targeted instruction to improve student performance and confidence in the content course.

3. Learning Communities

According to Peter Schmidt in the *Chronicle of Higher Education* (2008), academically underprepared students "benefit from being placed in effective learning communities where they take classes together and can give each other support."

Learning communities are defined as a group of students taking two or more courses together, forming a sort of study team (Tinto, 1998) and providing a comfortable, family-like learning environment for them. Tinto points out that if students are involved in the social and academic life of an institution, they are more likely to continue their education and to learn from it (1998). Because of their effectiveness, Learning Communities are growing in popularity among remedial learners and, more specifically, ESL learners. Kingsborough Community College in Brooklyn, New York, is considered to be a model for ESL learning communities. This program links five courses, including ESL, speech, a content course such as history or biology, and two developmental or life skills courses.

Other colleges and universities with successful learning communities for ESL students include Seattle Central Community College, LaGuardia Community College, and the University of Minnesota. In fact, the University of Minnesota offers one of the oldest learning community programs in the United States, incorporating writing, content-based learning, and learning communities. For 26 years, the Commanding English Program at Minnesota has connected language and academic support with college (content) coursework for Generation 1.5 students, who share in the learning experience together (Murie & Fitzpatrick, 2009). The focus of this program is on connection—"to other courses, services, advisors, and faculty in the college, so that the program responds to students in multiple ways" (p. 156). In other words, this two-semester program, one of the few that combines ESL and developmental coursework (Murie & Thomson, 2001), links courses and faculty in such a way so as to provide access to language and literacy through both the courses and the built-in support system. For DI students, learning communities can provide social connections with other students who, though from diverse backgrounds, may have had similar academic and family experiences. In addition, faculty in DI learning communities can work together to identify and address individual students' needs.

After exploring these approaches to teaching Generation 1.5 and other L2 students, the three faculty members at Penn State Brandywine decided to combine all three approaches, and, partnering with the campus leaning center, created the American Studies Cluster (ASC), targeting the twenty least academically prepared DI students on campus. The program began with a one-semester cluster of courses, using existing courses and course numbers, and it expanded to meet more and more of the students' needs.

The American Studies Cluster

The ASC is similar to other approaches in that it targets those immigrant students who are challenged by academic literacy skills and by the higher education experience in general. The ASC and programs like it are different from other approaches in that they are not just one approach but a collaboration of several approaches. Perhaps one aspect of the ASC that makes it special is that it is not only intended for developmental immigrant students; it was inspired by them. In other words, like other programs developed for students with special needs, faculty listened to students who were struggling academically and socially on campus and responded to their academic and social needs. Thus, this program has always been about the student.

Placement into the ASC begins the summer prior to the fall semester of students' first year. After prospective students take their entry exams, those who tested into developmental English classes are interviewed individually by the instructors in the learning center, who then identify students as second language learners, by looking at SAT scores and high school GPAs, and asking them what language is spoken at home and if they have difficulty in writing. The instructors then make recommendations on whether or not students should participate in the ASC. A second way of identifying students for the ASC is by self-identification (as a second language learner) on university entrance forms. Ironically, many second language students do not identify themselves as second language learners, a finding supported by Goen et al.'s (2001) survey of Generation 1.5 students who not only identified with the American culture but also who did not identify with ESL learners even though they were learners of English.

The learning center (LC) instructors then encourage those students who should participate in the program to do so. Instructors sometimes encounter resistance by students because of the stigma, in their mind, associated with "ESL" programs and because students don't want to be "segregated" from the larger student population. LC instructors explain to the students that each course within the cluster is a stand-alone course within the university's undergraduate degree curriculum (course names and numbers are the same for both ASC and mainstream courses: American Studies, English Rhetoric and Composition, etc.); no course is labeled ESL, and each course covers the same material as the mainstream courses (only with added support) taught at Penn State, which is one of the reasons why students don't think of this program as an ESL or developmental program. This student-involved scheduling process is in response to Harklau's (2000) charge that educators should engage students in program and placement decisions, and it entails a full explanation and discussion of the benefits of the program—a program that consists of students taking the same level courses as their American counterparts with the same autonomous nature of those courses (Harklau, 2000), but with a focus on non-native speakers and with additional built-in support systems to help these students succeed in college. Once the program is discussed with the students, most agree to participate in it and are enrolled in the cluster. See Figure 2.1 for the complete process of enrolling DI students into the ASC.

The ASC is comprised of a cluster of courses that weave students, faculty, cultures, and knowledge together. The courses work together in a fluid rather than linear fashion, with the first-year seminar providing the impetus in terms of offering a forum for students to debrief and synthesize ideas surrounding American culture, including those concerning the American system of higher education and these students' role within this system.

Table 2.1 summarizes the American Studies cluster of courses. (See Appendix 2a for a complete description of each course.)

The American Studies Cluster is just one approach to help DI students complete their undergraduate education. Records kept on every student who participates in the

FIGURE 2.1
American Studies Cluster Flow Chart

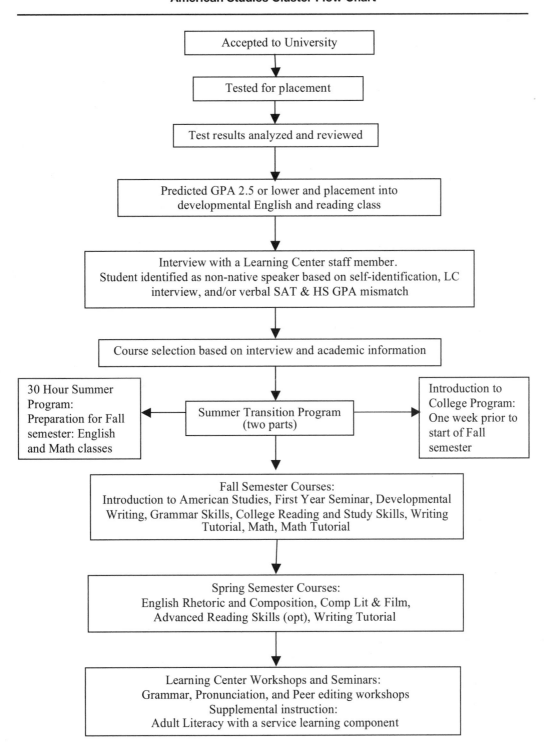

Accepted to University

Tested for placement

Test results analyzed and reviewed

Predicted GPA 2.5 or lower and placement into
developmental English and reading class

Interview with a Learning Center staff member.
Student identified as non-native speaker based on self-identification, LC
interview, and/or verbal SAT & HS GPA mismatch

Course selection based on interview and academic information

30 Hour Summer
Program:
Preparation for Fall
semester: English
and Math classes

Summer Transition Program
(two parts)

Introduction to
College Program:
One week prior to
start of Fall
semester

Fall Semester Courses:
Introduction to American Studies, First Year Seminar, Developmental
Writing, Grammar Skills, College Reading and Study Skills, Writing
Tutorial, Math, Math Tutorial

Spring Semester Courses:
English Rhetoric and Composition, Comp Lit & Film,
Advanced Reading Skills (opt), Writing Tutorial

Learning Center Workshops and Seminars:
Grammar, Pronunciation, and Peer editing workshops
Supplemental instruction:
Adult Literacy with a service learning component

TABLE 2.1
Courses and Programs in the American Studies Cluster
(See Appendix 2a for a description of these programs.)

Learning Center Summer Programs (Summer prior to first semester)
▪ 30-Hour Program
▪ Introduction to College Program (1 credit)
First Semester Courses: (Fall Semester)
▪ Introduction to American Studies (3 credits)
▪ College Reading and Study Skills I (3 credits)*
▪ Developmental Writing (Composition) (3 credits)*
▪ Introduction to English Grammar (3 credits)
▪ First-Year Seminar (no credit, credit tied to American Studies course)
▪ Weekly Writing Tutorial (1 credit)*
▪ (Math, course based on entry level exam) (3 or 4 credits)
▪ (Math tutorial-optional) (1 credit)
Second-Semester Courses: (Spring Semester)
▪ Developmental Writing (Composition) II, (if needed)* or College Rhetoric and Composition (3 credits)
▪ Comparative International Literature and Film (3 credits)
▪ Weekly writing tutorial (optional) (1 credit)*
▪ Math (sequential) (3 or 4 credits)
▪ (Math tutorial) (optional) (1 credit)
▪ College Reading and Study Skills II (if needed) (3 credits)*
▪ 1 or 2 Electives, student choice (3 credits each)
Enrichment Courses and Opportunities:
▪ Adult literacy with a service learning component (6 credits)
▪ Community service (1 to 3 credits)
▪ Undergraduate research

* Credits are factored into the GPA but do not count toward graduation

ASC suggest that the program has been effective for these students: GPAs are much higher than predicted and retention rates (between 96–100 percent) are much higher than the rates for the mainstream students on campus. Providing these statistics regularly to the Dean of Academics and citing them on grant applications has allowed the program to continue to grow. Certainly, the program would not be so effective if we did not have the support of both faculty and administration. Learning center instructors and ASC faculty continually foster personal relationships with campus faculty and administration to maintain this support, for both the program and the students. In return, faculty and administration support the program and its students by participating in the program itself (lecturing to DI students in their areas of expertise), and by participating in the multicultural programs these students organize.

Part II

Partnering with Campus Support Programs

Chapter 3

Supporting Classroom Learning:
The Learning Center

KEY POINTS

☞ Support services offered in learning centers can help to eliminate barriers to learning.

☞ Learning centers can provide a collaborative learning environment to enhance the academic achievement of developmental immigrant students.

Where can I get help with my English? I'm so frustrated.

—first-year developmental immigrant student

Colleges and universities throughout the United States offer valuable resources outside of the classroom to help students make the transition from high school to college, and to help them make their way through college. It is sometimes precisely because of the many services and personnel that support classroom efforts that developmental students, especially DI students, are able to graduate from college.

One crucial resource for developmental immigrant students can be found in campus learning centers. Learning Centers (also called Learning Assistance Centers, Academic Success Centers, Learning Skills Centers, Learning Laboratories, Centers for Academic Development, etc. [Stern, 2001]) enable immigrant students (and other underprepared students) to become more competent learners, and they enable teachers to advance their students' academic development.

Generally, learning centers offer a variety of academic support services that may include individualized or group support (workshops or study groups), developmental support (developmental courses), writing support, testing accommodation and preparation, reading assessment and tutorials, academic advising and counseling, and faculty and/or peer tutoring. In other words, most learning centers focus on working with students who need some extra help with their course work.

Of course, not all colleges and universities have a learning center, but rather a writing center, whose primary focus is to help students with their academic writing endeavors: understanding an assignment, getting started, getting organized, revising, proofreading, documenting sources, etc. On those campuses that have both a learning center and a writing center, the two centers often can and do overlap, but the underlying goals and audience are usually different: whereas the learning center usually targets remedial or developmental students, the writing center usually targets more traditional, non-developmental students. For those institutions with no learning center, most students will find the writing support they need in the writing center.

Research has shown that support services offered in learning centers eliminate barriers to learning (Gibbs, 1994) as they provide meaningful access to students from every background (Miksch et al., 2003) and promote student success (Starks, 1989). Through academic support, learning centers ultimately empower students to make informed decisions about and take responsibility for their own education.

The concept of academic support draws from Vygotsky's notion of scaffolding, where students can progress academically within a "temporary framework" that "supports [them] as they develop new skills" (Starr, 2000, p. 1). Scaffolding entails sequencing prompted content, materials, tasks, and teacher and peer support to optimize learning (Dickson, Chard, & Simmons, 1993) so that students can apply new skills and strategies on their own (Rosenshine & Meister, 1992). Vygotsky believed that mental processes are dependent on interactions with others (Vygotsky, 1978) and that there needs to be a way to connect what the students know and what they need to know. Vygotsky also believed that relationships between students and those that are more advanced in their thinking are central in developing learning and central to scaffolded instruction.

Through scaffolded instruction, learning center instructors and tutors promote academic literacy and, ultimately, help facilitate the success of DI students. Hogan and Pressley (1997) have identified five instructional scaffolding strategies that tutors can use in the learning center: modelling desired behaviors, offering explanations, inviting student participation, verifying and clarifying student understandings, and inviting student contribution (pp. 17–36). Each of these strategies can be used until the students are able to process new course material on their own. The ultimate goal in using these strategies is to provide just enough assistance to guide the students toward independence and self-sufficiency.

In conjunction with these strategies, Hogan and Pressley (1997) have identified effective scaffolding practices that tutors can use to promote this independence:

1. Diagnosing student needs and understandings: being knowledgeable of content and sensitive to the students (e.g., aware of the students' background knowledge and misconceptions) to determine if they are making progress.

2. Providing tailored assistance: using cueing or prompting, questioning, modelling, telling, or discussing to meet the students' needs.

3. Giving feedback: helping students learn to monitor their own progress by summarizing progress and noting behaviors that contribute to the student's success.

4. Controlling frustration and risk: creating an environment in which the students feel free to take risks with learning by encouraging them to try alternatives.

5. Assisting in internalization, independence, and generalization to other contexts: offering students the opportunity to practice a task in a variety of contexts.

This type of instruction is usually not found enough in the classroom because of class size or time constraints or because many content faculty are not trained in this type of instruction. As a result, individual struggles can get lost in the larger group, whereas tutors in learning centers, both professional tutors (sometimes they are adjunct English or ESL instructors as well as tutors) and peer (student) tutors, are able to address students' specific needs, reinforcing what is taught in the classroom so that successful outcomes can be achieved. In other words, learning centers provide academic support in ways that most classrooms cannot: an environment that offers individualized and group access to academic services in the form of content tutoring, peer mentoring, computer-assisted instruction, study skill instruction, advising, workshops, and study groups. In addition, and perhaps, more important, they offer a "sense of place" (Enright, 1997) that can help students reach their academic potential, one strategy at a time. Put simply, the strategies and skills taught by tutors in learning centers can promote the academic literacy necessary for academic success.

The Role of the Tutor and Developmental Immigrant Students

The learning center's supporting role in helping students achieve academic success is accomplished with some very dedicated professional tutors who can help all students with whatever difficulties they may face in their academic career. Most tutors serve the campus needs for reading and study support. However, in addition to assisting the entire campus, the learning center should have tutors dedicated specifically to the needs of DI students, who can also serve as a liaison between students and their instructors. Building a rapport and developing a partnership of trust is paramount to this relationship as the tutor and the DI students will be working very closely together for the first year. It is important that the tutor acknowledge the needs of the DI student and gets to know each student well. The tutor-tutee relationship should be one in which the student feels supported in tackling issues, comfortable in sharing problems and, ultimately, confident in taking risks.

In addition to professional tutors, many learning center tutors are peer tutors. At Penn State Brandywine, the peer tutors are upper class students who have maintained an A average in the subjects of English and/or math and who have demonstrated a dedication to the learning process by actively cultivating their own study skills and habits. They are recruited through teacher recommendation or by self-application in response to signs posted on campus towards the end of the spring semester. After they are hired and before the new semester begins, they attend an intensive one-week training session, in which they are trained by learning center staff to work with all populations of students, including DI students. During this time they meet with faculty from both the math and English departments to learn about instructors' skill expectations of first-year students on the first day of class. Tutors then receive hands-on instruction from learning center staff and review strategies for helping students prepare for their fall classes, such as time management and note-taking skills. They also participate in learning center meetings throughout the semester to discuss specific student-related issues, problems, and solutions such as parental and work pressure, student dissatisfaction or fear of doing poorly, and unusual skill needs or problems so that they can continually meet the needs of the students.

After the training session, peer tutors are responsible for keeping logs on all the students; evaluating, reviewing, and discussing all work done by them; and encouraging them to build upon strengths and improve weaknesses. These logs include assignments discussed and work done during the session. Though the primary goal of the tutors is to help strengthen the academic skills of their tutees, a secondary goal is to make the incoming students feel comfortable in both the learning center and the university environment by connecting with the students and giving them a student's view on the college experience.

DI students benefit greatly from the latter goal since many of them, especially at commuter campuses, rely on public transportation to get them to and from school during the school year and thus they spend long days on campus. The learning center becomes their "home" base and safe haven; it is the place where they do most of their work, somewhat like the "learning community" or "living learning center" described in Edwards and McKelfresh (2002).

Though learning center goals can vary from one institution to the next, many goals align closely with those discussed in the Teaching Study Skills/What to Expect in College and Reading chapters (including time management skills, oral language skills, reading support, etc.). Building on Hogan and Pressley's (1997) practices, this chapter offers additional suggestions on how learning centers can provide a collaborative learning environment to enhance the academic achievement of DI students.

Goal 1: Provide Writing Support

My writing is bad. If my writing improves, I will do good in college.

—first-year developmental immigrant student

Challenge

For many students, writing ultimately becomes the barrier that prevents them from completing their higher education. The struggles they encounter may be due to a variety of reasons, including a lack of formal academic writing instruction and a lack of first language literacy.

Suggested Approaches

Though many developmental students struggle with writing, developmental immigrant students have an especially difficult time with it. An important way for students to improve their academic writing proficiency is for them to take advantage of the support services that instructors or tutors in a learning center can provide.

■ **For students who struggle with writing, it is important that they meet with a learning center instructor or tutor at least once a week (and more often during weeks when important papers are due).**

It is advantageous for students to see the same tutor on a regular basis to maximize the student's time and effort spent in the learning center. (See previous section on how to find good peer tutors.) A tutor gets to know and understand a student's writing problems, and the student feels comfortable and 'safe' with the same writing tutor. The tutor also understands what the student is trying to express, both orally and in written form, as he/she becomes familiar with the student's particular way of speaking and writing. For example, a tutor knows that with some students, using incorrect tenses is a common error in their writing. This knowledge contributes to much less frustration on the part of both the DI student and the tutor. On the other hand, when students see different tutors, it usually results in the tutors only focusing on grammatical problems and not on the thinking behind the ideas, whereas a tutor dedicated to DI students is able to engage in deeper conversations, which in turn, helps students gain control of their writing. An excellent resource for helping DI students with their writing problems is Reynolds' *One on One with Second Language Writers* (2009).

■ **Good communication between writing instructors and learning center tutors helps tutors determine how to best help students.**

It is important that tutors are knowledgeable about writing topics assigned by various instructors as well as the due dates for specific papers (having the student bring a copy of each assignment or having a syllabus for each of a student's courses helps). Also, when DI students are struggling with a concept in their reading or writing, the tutor can explain this to the instructors who can adjust their teaching accordingly, if they choose to. Because of the nature of college coursework, an instructor often does not recognize that a problem exists until an exam or paper is due. By then it may be too late; the student might get a low grade and become discouraged. If, however, the tutor notes that there is a problem and alerts the instructor, the problem can be averted.

■ **Tutors can serve students well by reinforcing, clarifying, and modelling writing strategies taught in the classroom.**

Explanations of writing strategies (such as brainstorming and using graphic organizers) taught in writing classes enable students to better understand these strategies and to practice using them with the tutor. Additional class-based information can also be explained and modelled: formatting the five paragraph essay, writing topic sentences and thesis statements, writing different types of essays, editing papers, and writing rough drafts versus writing finished essays. (Again, upper class tutors have taken many of the courses that they are tutoring the DI students in, and they have been trained to use these writing strategies during the tutorials.)

■ **Tutors can help students learn how to edit their own essays.**

Tutors should reemphasize the reading-writing connection. Students become better writers when they learn to move from writing their papers to reading their papers. Students should understand that essay writing and other types of formal papers usually require more than one draft: after writing the first draft, the student then becomes a reader, then a writer, then a reader, and so forth, until the final draft is written. Reworked and rewritten drafts generally lead to more effective essays.

■ **Tutors can show students how to sift through research to find what they are looking for in order to cite it for a research paper.**

Doing research and writing research papers can overwhelm DI students. By discussing the research process and breaking it down into manageable parts, the tutor can help students move through the process with relative ease.

■ **Tutors can clarify what plagiarism is and show how to cite sources accurately.**

Tutors can give students examples and have students practice citing sources.

Goal 2: Help Students Learn Project Coordination

After two months I started to understood little bit working with tutor.

—first-year developmental immigrant student

Challenge

Many DI students are overwhelmed when confronted with a group project because they have little or no previous experience with larger projects or group efforts and are often not comfortable asserting themselves as a group.

Suggested Approaches

The learning center tutor is able to break down the project into manageable chunks for these students by advising them where to start and how to proceed from there. Presenting material in small steps enables students to manage the project and learn from it. The tutor can help students make a checklist of what needs to be done and a realistic timeframe for doing each task. The tutor can serve as a verbal reminder to students to help them stay on task and to make sure that each task is completed by certain dates.

■ **The tutor can help the student practice oral presentations, utilizing PowerPoint and other media, and assist with the research process or any other written parts of the project.**

Tutors can provide valuable feedback to students if students practice their presentations with them.

■ **The tutor can facilitate application to other situations.**

Because so many courses assign topic-specific group projects, it is advantageous to capitalize on these topics by using them as springboards for other class assignments to enhance academic literacy. Some of these activities include debating the topic (such as affirmative action in a history or American Studies class) and writing a persuasive essay on the same topic (in an English class). By breaking down projects and by building upon project topics, learning center staff can equip DI students with valuable tools to use in the classroom and beyond. Because students can practice projects in a safe setting where they are free to make mistakes, and because they are with someone who can give honest and meaningful pointers on what could be improved, the students present a better project, which can ultimately lead to a higher grade.

Goal 3: Provide a Contact Person to Help Students Solve Problems

---

I'm in college and a freshman, too. I have talk to a lot of my freshman because without them you feel that you are in the twilight zone.

—first-year developmental immigrant student

Challenge

DI students need to know that they have a 'safe haven' within the university in which to go when they need help. Even more importantly, they need to know that there is someone in this place that they can always turn to when help is needed. This person serves as a contact person for the student: someone who knows about the student's courses (has all the course syllabi), knows the student's needs in terms of academic literacy skills, and, in some ways, becomes the student's confidant.

Suggested Approaches

While ALL tutors that work with DI students can be/need to be advocates, having one point person is recommended. This point person is dedicated to this group of students, meeting with each of the students at least once a week. This tutor will be the person that advocates for the students and helps the students learn to advocate for themselves.

There are many challenges confronting tutors who work with developmental immigrant students. One is that they must get to know and develop a rapport with each of the students. The tutor, in the one-on-one process of meeting with the students every week, gets to know each student as an individual in a way that is sometimes difficult for classroom professors. It is within the context of this dialogue that the tutor gets to know some of the personal struggles that the student faces. The tutor also comes to recognize the unique learning style and/or difficulties of the student. A DI student's individual learning difficulties may get overlooked in high schools. Many learning problems are lumped together as a language learning problem: the student is still struggling with learning English when, in fact, there may be an underlying learning disability that has not been recognized. This is where it becomes clear that the tutor needs to be a person who is concerned with and understands the unique problems of this population so that a learning difficulty can be distinguished from learning a language.

The tutor's knowledge of the student goes beyond identifying problems with course work. A tutor is the person who knows who has been in the country for only two years, who went to a high school in a lower socioeconomic community, and who is responsible for doing all the translating in their families. The above are common examples of what DI students deal with. In fact, some of the students deal with all of these issues: mastering English after being in the United States for a short time, beginning university after completing their secondary education at a disadvantaged high school, and doing the bulk of the translating for the family.

Tutors in undergraduate learning centers play a crucial role in the education of developmental immigrant students. They supplement classroom learning by providing a support system that helps students reach their educational goals. Whether the learning center tutor is an instructor or a peer, each has a repertoire of effective learning strategies to pass on to students and each contributes to the students' ultimate success.

Chapter 4

Teaching Study Skills and What to Expect in College

KEY POINTS

- Many developmental immigrant students are unsure about college expectations or academic demands in higher education.

- The more information that students have about expectations and demands at the beginning of their college experience, the more rewarding their experience will be.

- Developmental immigrant students need to learn effective study skills to handle the increased challenges they will face in college.

I really don't know what to expect from college.

Do professors take attendance?

This semester I'm taking 15 credits and plan to work 30 hours per week at my job.

—first-year developmental immigrant students

In addition to learning centers, many undergraduate colleges and universities offer orientation programs or summer bridge programs to help students acclimate to the college environment. It is often in these programs that students figure out whether the campus community will be a good fit for them or not; their first impression is a most important one, one that could impact their overall educational experience. It is also in these programs where developmental students, especially DI students, are made aware of the many people who are willing to help them become a vibrant part of the campus community (through clubs, sports, etc.) and to help them navigate their way through the college system.

Because DI students are often the first in their families to attend a U.S. university, they really don't know what to expect from higher education (Roberge, 2009), other than its being a path to a high-paying or prestigious job (Brooks-Terry, 1988). Many envision a sort of 13th grade, a place where grades are linked to effort (and not necessarily to a final product) and where students can always turn a failing grade into a passing one by doing extra credit or by handing in a stack of late assignments on the last day.

Many DI students and their parents believe that it is the university's job (and not necessarily the students') to ensure that students receive an education (Goldschmidt & Ousey, 2006). In this way, education is *passive*, "given" to students who simply complete assignments, instead of *active*, where students take control of and are responsible for their own learning. Thus, it can take students a semester or more to realize that college requires different skills and approaches from those required in high school (Goldschmidt & Ousey, 2006). By teaching about the expectations of college and study skills early (ideally, before the first semester begins) and continuing to emphasize the expectations throughout the semester, instructors can help DI students achieve a strong first semester and a good start to their college careers. Former DI students (current sophomores, juniors, and seniors) can also be instrumental guides to incoming first-year DI students.

The following goals and activities can be used in summer orientation programs, bridge programs, first-year seminars, or other introduction to college programs and can allow DI students to better understand college expectations, study skills, and their role as college students.

Goal 1: Help Students Better Understand the Expectations of College Instructors

---

You mean professors don't give extra credit?

—*first-year developmental immigrant student*

Challenge

Many DI students are used to having personal relationships with high school teachers who "go the extra mile" for these "determined, hardworking, and even inspirational students" (Harklau, 2000), and they expect similar relationships with teachers in college. However, not all college instructors meet individually with students; if they do, it is generally not to help with language-related problems. Students with language problems are often "handed over" to the campus learning or writing centers by instructors who are overwhelmed and perplexed by the grammatical and language errors in the students' written work (Zamel, 1995). Unsure of the new rules in an academic environment where performance, not simply effort, matters, DI students have difficulty adapting to the new academic demands. They are soon frustrated and confused; after all, they earned high grades in their high school classes and were admitted into college or university.

Suggested Approaches

DI students can greatly benefit from specific instruction on professors' expectations. These discovery and discussion activities can provide students with information about expectations that can help them succeed from the start of their higher education.

■ **Teach students how to examine and understand a syllabus.**

A college syllabus is a contract between the professor and the student. Students can examine their "contracts" from different classes in detail, either individually or in pairs or small groups, to better understand class expectations. One example is to create a checklist for helping them understand a syllabus, such as looking at how much reading is required, how many exams there are, and how much writing is required. (A sample checklist is included in Appendix 4a.) The knowledge gained can then be used in the time management section's activities (see Goal 4).

■ **Help students brainstorm questions to ask instructors and then give them an opportunity to practice asking them in an informal setting.**

DI students are often uncomfortable approaching professors with questions, either during or after class. By inviting professors of first-semester classes into a summer Introduction to College Program (or other summer orientation programs) for an informal lunch and/or discussion, instructors can create a more comfortable environment for discussion. If students have previously examined syllabi (especially of the professor visiting the class), instructors can put them into small groups or work as a class to brainstorm questions and put them on the board. The listed questions can be good starting points for this informal discussion.

■ **Facilitate discussions between new and returning students.**

Inviting former DI students (who are current sophomores, juniors, or seniors) to talk with new DI students in a program during the summer or in the first week of the semester can give the new students an opportunity to ask questions, get tips and advice, and meet possible mentors to help them during their first year. Students can brainstorm questions ahead of time. Allowing this discussion to occur without the instructor present can add a much-needed level of candor.

■ **Provide college scenarios for discussion.**

Former DI students (or the instructor) can also lead a role-playing exercise in which students are given scenarios ("You have to take your brother to the doctor and will have to miss class," "You're having a hard time understanding your math professor because she talks quickly") and then discuss possible solutions with a classmate or in a group. The books *100 Things Every College Student Ought to Know* (Disbro, 1996) and *College Knowledge: 101 Tips* (Schoem, 2005) have been used effectively at Penn State Brandywine to spark discussion between incoming and former DI students. Incoming DI students can look through these books individually, in pairs, or in small groups and mark or list the information that they found most surprising or that they would like to know more about. Students can also write reflectively on what they already knew, what surprised them, and what they would like to know more about. Former DI students or the instructor can then respond to this knowledge orally and/or in writing.

■ **Provide clear tips about what to do for the first day in all classes.**

Sit toward the front. Look interested. Bring a notebook, pen, and the textbook, as professors will start teaching on the first day. Get some type of weekly planner. Tips such as these can be invaluable to incoming DI students, and discussing them with students before or on the first day of the fall semester can help them be better prepared for all their classes.

■ **Develop a semester-long dialogue on "What is a good education?"**

By developing their own thoughts on this topic, students can incorporate the values they experience in various college classrooms and compare them to the values that they currently hold. Video clips such as the Pink Floyd music video "Another Brick in the Wall" (available on YouTube; lyrics available elsewhere online), excerpts of classroom scenes from the movie *Ferris Bueller's Day Off* (1986), a reading of the poem "Sick" (which begins "I cannot go to school today. . .") by Shel Silverstein (available online), or readings from Ruth Spack's *Guidelines* (2007) have been used as prompts on our campus to begin a discussion of the roles of students' and teachers' attitudes and expectations of education.

■ **Help students explore expectations and requirements of their intended majors.**

Many DI students and their parents view college as the means to a prestigious job, which to them is often in medicine, business, or the sciences. Goldschmidt and Seifried (2008) found that 85 percent of DI students entering Penn State Brandywine expected to pursue a career in medicine, business, or engineering, but their combined SAT scores averaged 717. Goldschmidt and Ousey (2006) note that "it is not at all unusual for a student to be placed in a developmental math class, do poorly, and sometimes fail it, yet want to become a doctor or engineer, or for a student to fail Biology I, yet want to become a nurse" (p. 18). Many times DI students do not know what course of study is required for their desired professions, expressing surprise that a medical degree requires eight years of study plus a residency, or that nursing requires many science courses. One way to help DI students set clear professional and academic goals is to work with them to explore career possibilities and course requirements for intended careers. They could do this by visiting the career center, using various career websites, or researching and writing a paragraph or essay on the process of attaining their specific career goal.

■ **Familiarize students with online campus resources.**

During the summer or in the first week of classes, especially in a first-year seminar class, DI students can be introduced to online databases by providing them with a list of current event topics and having them find relevant articles. A summer program can utilize campus email accounts and Blackboard or another course management system, so that students are comfortable with these tools when classes begin in the fall. Students could also be introduced to other campus online resources that post grades, progress reports, or courses required for the major.

Goal 2: Help Students Discover Their Own Strengths, Weaknesses, and Attitudes with the Help of Peer Tutors or Peer Mentors

---

I'm bad at grammer.

I think I will do good in college.

—first-year developmental immigrant students

Challenge

DI students have often not reflected on their own specific strengths, weaknesses, and attitudes, either assuming that because they did well in high school, they will do well in college (Goldschmidt & Ousey, 2006), or generalizing their weaknesses in blanket statements such as, "I don't like to read" or "I can't write." Students usually cannot articulate what grammatical issues they find troublesome; they often simply view themselves as "bad at" all grammar in a hopeless way. They don't realize how their attitudes toward writing or reading can affect their ability to learn, or that these attitudes can be changed as they gain skills, as they ask for help, and as assignments are broken into pieces and made more manageable.

Suggested Approaches

DI students can benefit greatly from interaction with peer tutors or mentors. These tutors (ideally sophomore, junior, or senior former DI students) can help them envision what they can become. In addition, a summer program before the start of their first year in a campus learning or writing center can create mentor relationships before the semester even begins and make the learning center a natural "landing pad" for students during the first weeks of the semester (Goldschmidt, Notzold, & Ziemba-Miller, 2003). A checklist of suggested activities for a summer peer tutoring program is shown in Figure 4.1. Students can track their progress and evaluate themselves based on the checklist. The activities listed can help DI students see that reading and writing are skills that can be developed and enjoyed. Most important, working with peer tutors allows DI students to see what type of students they can develop into and what steps they need to take to reach that goal.

■ **Begin a summer program or orientation with an entrance interview.**

An entrance interview (a sample is available in Appendix 4b) can reveal college expectations; help get DI students thinking about and articulating their strengths, weaknesses, hopes and fears; and begin to make students more comfortable asking for help when needed. This works best as part of a discussion in which the peer tutor asks the questions, writes the results and discusses them, shares personal experiences, and asks follow-up questions as needed. This type of give-and-take builds relationships and allows DI students to view the tutors as people they can trust.

■ **Survey students about their feelings about entering the campus.**

Discussing the results of a survey (a sample is available in Appendix 4b) on their feelings about different academic skills with peer tutors can help DI students explore their own attitudes. Tutors and DI students can discuss causes and possible remedies for negative feelings and build on positive feelings, and tutors can share their own feelings from their first year. Reexamining answers on the survey at the end of a summer program or orientation course can show students how their feelings have changed once they have learned more about the college experience.

■ **Provide students with college-level vocabulary awareness.**

The Academic Word List (AWL) (Coxhead, 1998 & 2000) is a list of words that occur frequently in academic texts across the disciplines. Exposing students to these words can help set the expectations for college-level reading and help students see how much they may need to develop their vocabulary. DI students and their tutors can work through online AWL exercises together. Students can also practice editing for word choice by circling three to five words in their own written paragraphs that they would like to improve and then choosing a stronger or more precise word with an online thesaurus or thesaurus tool. Because discussions about word choice are so important, peer tutors can help clarify meanings and help DI students see

FIGURE 4.1
30-Hour Summer Program Checklist of Completed Activities

MATH COURSE_____   ENGLISH COURSE_____

NAME_____

1) Initial Interview_____   General Survey A _____

2) Suggested Summer Reading List_____

ENGLISH Diagnostic Paragraph_____

3) Introduction to proofreading sheet and English tips list _____

4) English Paragraph 1 _____

5) English Paragraph 2 _____

6) English Paragraph 3 _____

7) Grammar Diagnostic Pre _____   Post _____

8) Grammar Exercises _____

9) Thesaurus Worksheets 1_____ 2_____ 3_____ 4 _____ 5_____

10) Vocabulary worksheet 1 _____ 2_____ 3_____ 4_____ 5 _____

11) Vocabulary Quiz _____

12) Transition words worksheet _____

13) Online grammar tutorial _____

MATH Math Diagnostic Pre-test score _____   Post-test score_____

14) Math Worksheets Completed ____ ____ ____ ____ ____ ____ ____ ____

15) Math Anxiety video_____ Math tips _____ Math formulas _____

16) Math Quizzes ____ ____ ____ ____ ____ ____ ____

17) Math Post-Test Review _____

OTHER LEARNING ACTIVITIES

18) Reading Discussions Completed ____ ____ ____ ____ ____

19) Goal Setting Sheet _____

20) Learning Channel Preference _____

21) Learning Style Inventory _____

22) Online database search _____

23) Coping with Your First Year discussion _____

FINAL ASSESSMENT

24) Final Evaluation Completed _____

25) General Survey B _____

26) Exit Interview _____

Created by Norma Notzold and the Penn State Brandywine Learning Center. Used with permission.

that English-English tools often provide better word choices than foreign language dictionaries can. Selecting only a few words to change is important to ensure that the final product doesn't read like a thesaurus, but rather is a more exact expression of ideas. Sharing their revised paragraphs with other DI students, peer tutors, and/or instructors can help students judge their improvement.

■ **Provide students with an awareness of college reading demands.**

Incoming DI students can benefit from a review of the concepts of topic and main idea, as these are critical to college reading success. Again, peer tutors can model thinking strategies and discuss their own reading strategies. Peer tutors can show DI students common introductory college textbooks and discuss pre-reading, reading, and study strategies and how to use textbook companion websites.

■ **Provide students with grammar diagnostic pre- and post-tests.**

A good grammar diagnostic can help DI students view their strengths, focus on the specific grammatical issues that give them difficulty, and prioritize their errors when editing. Excellent free grammar diagnostics and exercises tailored to students' results are available on the Internet. Grammar instruction is discussed in more detail in Chapter 9.

■ **Provide information during the summer about academic writing expectations.**

Peer tutors or other orientation leaders can talk about the writing expectations of college composition courses. The writing center can usually offer revising/editing checklists so that DI students have a sense of what to expect in their writing classes. Such information may encourage them to seek help early in the semester or whenever it is needed.

Goal 3: Help Students Identify and Use Their Own Learning Styles

I don't know what my learning style is.

—*first-year developmental immigrant student*

Challenge

Learning styles have been categorized in many ways; perhaps one of the most commonly known and used is the VARK model (Fleming, 2001), which includes the categories of Visual, Auditory, Reading/Writing preference, and Kinesthetic learners. DI students often believe that any learning difficulties they may have are solely attributed to language issues. Because many students have focused their efforts on acquiring English, they may not have ever examined how they study and learn or what their individual learning styles are.

Suggested Approaches

Several studies (Dunn, Honigsfeld, & Doolan, 2009; Rochford, 2004; Peacock, 2001) have found that when teachers adapt their teaching to students' learning styles, student performance improves. Instructors of DI students should try to accommodate multiple learning styles in their lessons, using methods and activities such as those described in Dunn & Griggs (2000). Studies have also shown that teaching students about learning styles and helping them discover their own styles (Nelson et al., 1993; Dunn & Dunn, 1993) increases student performance and retention. Helping students discover and understand their learning styles will assist them throughout their college careers and beyond. By thinking about how they learn best, DI students can begin to take control of their own learning.

- **Provide opportunities to take learning style quizzes.**

Many websites offer quick and useful online learning style quizzes students can take that offer instant test results and study tips based on these results. Some useful free quizzes can be found in the websites listed at the end of this chapter.

- **Help students think beyond the VARK model to other factors that affect learning.**

The Dunn & Dunn Learning-Style Model quiz (www.learningstyles.net), which costs $5 per test, provides 20 pages of individualized, detailed information and study tips based on Dunn & Dunn's (1993) 21 elements divided into five strands (environment, emotionality, sociological preferences, physiological preferences, and cognitive processing inclinations). Our campus has used Eric Jenson's book *Student Success Secrets* (2003), an accessible and motivational read that helps students think about their own learning and the various factors (similar to those in the Dunn & Dunn model) that influence their academic performance.

- **Work with students to brainstorm and try out learning strategies based on their learning style results.**

Students can share their learning style quiz results and work in groups (based on their styles) to brainstorm strategies (both from the suggestions the quiz results give and from the list) that work for them already or that they would like to try. Or, individually, students can look at the tips that come with their results and circle the strategies that they already use and that work for them and put a star next to strategies they'd like to try.

■ **Discuss different teaching styles and how to adapt to them.**

Some instructors write detailed outlines on PowerPoint, while others scribble a few key words on the board. Some lecture with no visuals, while some are more hands-on or use many learning modes simultaneously (seeing, hearing, doing). First-year seminar (FYS) instructors or peer tutors can discuss college instructors' teaching styles thus far (this is best if done a few weeks into the semester), and brainstorm together how students can adapt to these styles.

Goal 4: Explicitly Teach Time Management Skills

I don't use a planner.

—first-year developmental immigrant student

Challenge

Time management is a skill that college students identify as "critical to college readiness" (Byrd & MacDonald, 2005), and professors and researchers agree (Collier & Morgan, 2007; Conley, 2007). This skill, and the more general "student self management" of time and assignments (Conley, 2007), are skills that should be explicitly taught to incoming college students (such as in a FYS class), particularly to those students who are the first in their generation to attend an American college (Collier & Morgan, 2007). However, Collier and Morgan found that even when professors verbally emphasized the time commitment requirements of their courses' assignments, "according to both first-generation and traditional students, their time commitments inevitably reflected the amount of time available, rather than the amount of time it would take to master the course material" (p. 435). This becomes particularly problematic for DI students, who usually have more work and family responsibilities than "traditional" students, and who usually require additional time and support when working on assignments and readings.

Suggested Approaches

DI students should not only be told the time demands of college work, but they should also be able to see these demands in a hands-on, relevant way early in the semester as well as throughout the year (again, this could be done in a FYS class), so that they don't fall irretrievably behind. In that way, a student who earns a poor grade can start to think, "I need to better manage my time and use the learning center more," rather than "I can't do this" (Goldschmidt & Ousey, 2006).

■ **Assist students in planning out their time.**

It is generally recommended that for every hour that students are in class, they should spend two to three hours outside of class studying, reading, or working on the course. For students taking 15 credits, this means 30–45 hours each week should be blocked out for coursework. A good way to help students visualize this commitment is to ask them to complete a weekly schedule. Students should block in their classes, any employment commitments (more than 12 hours/week of outside employment can negatively affect grades), and time for meals, sleep, and exercise. They should then block in study times, paying attention to when and where they study best (mornings? on campus? right after class?) and create small, realistic chunks of study time. No eight-hour marathon study sessions on Saturdays are allowed on the schedule; this needs to be realistic! Students can then discuss their schedules and offer their reasoning behind their plans. They should also try out the schedule for a week or two and revise it as needed.

■ **Work as a class on breaking a large assignment into steps.**

After students have examined syllabi, they may be overwhelmed by the amount of reading per week or the number of upcoming papers. A class discussion or group work on breaking these assignments into manageable steps (a weekly 40-page reading load could be read as 10 pages on Monday, 10 on Tuesday, etc., or Section 3a on Monday, 3b on Tuesday, etc.; a three-page paper can be broken into brainstorming/planning one day, writing a draft the next day, etc.). Students can then write their more manageable tasks in their student planners.

■ **Work with students to use student planners effectively.**

The Student Life Office at many campuses gives out free weekly planners during orientation week. These often come with important campus dates and deadlines already added. Weekly planners can also be found in dollar stores, office supply stores and, of course, the campus bookstore. In the fall semester, instructors of Reading or Study Skills or FYS classes, for example, can make these planners a requirement of the course.

Goal 5: Explicitly Teach Key Study Skills

I studied, but I still failed.

There's so much to study. I don't know where to start.

—first-year developmental immigrant students

Challenge

DI students often enter college not realizing that they do not have the study skills necessary to succeed in college courses. They usually have never been taught study skills specifically and need to gain these skills quickly once they enter the university.

Suggested Approaches

DI students need direct instruction in and practice with study skills. These skills can be introduced in a summer orientation program or FYS class, but they need to be integrated into other courses (such as a reading or a content course) in order for students to be successful. The learning center can also reinforce these skills throughout the semester.

■ **Offer a one-credit study skills course during the regular semester.**

Dedicating time to explore how to learn can be extremely beneficial to students. Penn State Brandywine offers a half-semester, one credit study skills class (a course offered to all students, not just DI students, which is usually taken by students who had to drop a course and need to add a course to maintain full-time status). Texts that we have used in this course at Penn State Brandywine include Eric Jenson's student-friendly book *Student Success Secrets* (2003), which introduces practical tips for studying and learning. David Conley's *College Knowledge: What It Really Takes for Students to Succeed and What We Can Do to Get Them Ready* (2005) is a good resource for instructors.

■ **Provide an opportunity for DI students to assess their current study skills.**

Online study skills surveys can allow students to assess themselves. One example can be found at http://artchavez.net/survey.

■ **Provide instruction and practice in note-taking strategies.**

Many online sites offer tips for taking notes in college. One such site is Dartmouth's Academic Success Center (www.dartmouth.edu/~acskills/success/index.html). Its "Taking Lecture and Class Notes" link contains useful handouts on taking lecture notes and on the Cornell method of note taking. Jenson's (2003) chapter on note taking suggests that students vary the size of the words they write; use symbols and meaningful abbreviations; create charts, diagrams, and clusters; and draw memorable pictures. A useful way for students to try out these suggestions is to have them take notes on a lecture, such as Randy Pausch's "Last Lecture" (available on YouTube). Students can take notes on several minutes of the lecture and then meet in groups to compare their note taking. In this way, they can assess if they've included the important information, see which sets of notes are the easiest to read and study, and determine what note-taking tips work best for them.

■ **Provide an opportunity for students to research and teach study skills they want to learn.**

Students in a study skills or FYS class can be required to research a particular study skill that they want to learn more about, and then teach this skill to the class and provide a one-page handout of tips. Possible topics include how to memorize, how to study for a test, how to take tests (multiple choice, essay, etc.), how to avoid procrastination, how to manage stress, how to read a textbook, and how to manage time.

Goal 6: Introduce Students to Campus Resources in a Personal Way

They didn't talk about that at orientation . . . .

—first-year developmental immigrant student

Challenge

Because they are often the first in their family to attend a U.S. college or university, DI students have different questions about the experience than other students do, and sometimes they don't even know what to ask. Lacking the cultural capital that many students whose parents attended U.S. universities have, DI students must learn the "culture of the academy" (Kimmel & Davis, 1996) more explicitly as they enter their first year.

Suggested Approaches

A more personal and detailed introduction to the campus is necessary for DI students to feel comfortable and to make use of necessary resources. With this increased knowledge and familiarity, DI students can begin to develop "self-advocacy" (Notbohm,

2008) by recognizing when they need help and asking for help when they need it, which are critical skills for college success.

■ Provide an informal walking tour for students.

DI students sometimes find that campus orientations don't show everything that they need to see to the extent they need to see it. Instructors or peer tutors can take DI students (as part of a summer orientation or first-year seminar class) on a walking tour of the campus, being sure to walk through professors' office areas. (DI students are then more comfortable walking through them afterward. Many campus tours just "peek" into this area, making it feel taboo.) Students can be given a map with key items listed (advising office, study lounge, microwave, etc.), and each item can be pointed out during the tour.

■ Try a scavenger hunt.

Students can become more familiar with various campus offices (Advising, Finance, Records, etc.) by being paired up and given scavenger hunts of things to find. Items could include a drop-add form, a schedule of campus speakers, answers to specific questions, or signatures from various staff members. Instructors should work with campus staff so they expect the visits and students can get to know staff members personally. Of course, a prize for the first to complete the scavenger hunt can be an incentive to the activity.

■ Invite key campus staff members for a discussion over lunch.

Such an informal environment allows students to ask questions and learn more details than in a traditional orientation. Key staff members should come from offices like financial aid, advising, or the registrar.

Goal 7: Teach Students Financial Skills

Many of my students who struggle with working 20–30 hours a week at a part-time job while in school full time are the same ones who buy $10 lunches and $1.50 sodas every day on campus.

—*instructor of first-year developmental immigrant students*

Challenge

Unfortunately, many students come to campus with very little experience in managing money. Many DI students have part-time jobs (Roberge, 2009) (often working well beyond the 12 hours per week that is commonly recommended for academic success), and many have financial obligations (to contribute to the family and/or to pay their own expenses) that other college students may not have.

College students need to treat college as a full-time job; it certainly requires much more than 40 hours of effort each week for success. Therefore, it is critical that students learn how to manage their money wisely. Good financial choices may mean that students can work fewer hours at an outside job and have more time to devote to academics.

Suggested Approaches

It is critical that students think about their finances in a very concrete, hands-on way, where they can see how good financial management can lead to academic success. Providing students with the tools and knowledge to better handle their financial lives can have a large impact in the classroom and is critical for some students' success.

■ **Work with students to calculate the effects of incidental expenses.**

If you spend $1.50 on a soda from the vending machine every day, that's $7.50 a week or $142.50 for a 15-week semester (spent only on soda). How many hours do you need to work to earn $142.50? Sharing such simple math with students can have an eye-opening effect. Students quickly see that small changes make big financial differences and perhaps a difference on how many hours they need to work at their part-time jobs. *A 12-can case of soda is often on sale for $2.50 at the grocery store. That's less than 21 cents a can, or $1.05 per week or $15.75 per semester, a savings of $126.75.* Students can be taught how trimming expenses can lead to huge savings over time. David Bach's Latte Factor calculator (found online at www.finishrich.com/free_resources/fr_lattefactor.php) can illustrate how investing small amounts of money instead of spending it on daily incidentals (in his example, a latte and a muffin) can lead to future wealth and less financial struggle. Again, less struggle can mean more time devoted to academics and a more balanced life.

■ **Provide tools for students to keep track of spending.**

DI students should be encouraged to keep track of their spending for a week (or longer). They can keep a record of expenses on a sticky note in their wallets and then create a simple budget chart that tracks their expenses in various categories. At the end of the week, students could report on their results (they don't need to divulge exact numbers) and what categories they hope to cut back in.

■ **Provide students with online college budgeting resources.**

Many websites offer college budgeting times, printable budget worksheets, and other tools. Instructors can visit bankrate.com, youngmoney.com, or a similar site, and search for "college students" for a variety of articles and videos, or visit studentfinancialdomain.com for articles and advice for students. Adding these links to a class web page can allow students easy access to the information throughout the semester.

■ **Discuss ways to purchase textbooks economically.**

Former DI students can talk with current students about ways to purchase books online on sites such as book.ly, Amazon.com, and half.com. (It is crucial to find out the ISBN number of the text used in class, so the correct edition is bought online; it's also important to question the seller to be sure that an instructor's edition isn't purchased.) Sometimes ordering direct from the publisher is less expensive for students as well. They can also discuss ways students can sell their books on their own at the end of the semester or by accessing a campus book co-op.

■ **Discuss the perils of plastic.**

Every semester, credit card companies, offering free t-shirts or other incentives to students who sign up for a card, set up shop on many campuses. Former DI students, financial aid staff, or the instructor of an Introduction to College or a first-year seminar class can discuss and calculate the ramifications of taking on credit card debt in college. Many banks also offer to send in a staff member (for free) to discuss personal finance and budgeting with students.

■ **Personally introduce students to campus financial aid staff.**

An informal meeting or presentation can help students discuss money management and financial aid issues in a more personalized and in-depth way and will help DI students feel more comfortable meeting with financial aid staff on their own in the future. Students can also learn about work-study opportunities at this meeting.

■ **Level the playing field.**

Sometimes commuting DI students do not have computers at home and therefore must complete all computer-based work on campus. "If you don't live on campus, do you have a computer at home?" can easily be added to any first day of class survey. Partnering with the campus IT department may allow instructors to help fill this student need. Old computers can be collected from faculty or businesses (or even from the campus if it is upgrading), refurbished by IT staff or students, and given to students who need them.

When DI students learn about college expectations in an orientation class the summer before the fall semester or in a FYS class during their first semester, they stand a better chance of having a successful first year of college. Introducing DI students to these expectations in personal, meaningful, concrete ways can help them have a positive and meaningful college experience.

Additional Useful Websites

- **Vocabulary Exercises for the Academic Word List**
  www.academicvocabularyexercises.com
  Online exercises and information on Avril Coxhead's Academic Word List

- **Education Planner**
  www.educationplanner.com
  Includes a good learning style quiz

- **The VARK Learning Style Quiz**
  www.vark-learn.com

- **The Gregorc Style Delineator**
  www.thelearningweb.net/personalthink.html

Part III

Teaching Academic Literacy within an Academic Framework: Suggested Approaches

Chapter 5

Teaching Academic Integrity

KEY POINTS

☞ Many developmental immigrant students are not directly taught the writing conventions for working with sources.

☞ For most developmental immigrant students, the issue of plagiarism is not one of academic dishonesty or even necessarily a lack of understanding of conventions once they are taught them, but rather a need for advanced academic reading, writing, vocabulary, and grammatical skills that they do not yet possess.

. . . Academic integrity includes a commitment to not engage in or tolerate acts of falsification, misrepresentation or deception. Such acts of dishonesty include cheating or copying, plagiarizing, submitting another persons' work as one's own, using Internet sources without citation, fabricating field data or citations, "ghosting" (taking or having another student take an exam), stealing examinations, tampering with the academic work of another student, facilitating other students' acts of academic dishonesty, etc. . . .

—*from Penn State University Senate Policy 49-20*

Academic integrity is a much-discussed topic in higher education today and an increasingly legal one. Professors are often required to include campus academic integrity policy on their syllabi, and universities increasingly use plagiarism detection software such as TurnItIn (turnitin.com) and have elaborate judicial systems in place for students suspected of academic dishonesty. Academic integrity includes clear-cut issues such as copying another student's answers on a test or purchasing a term paper from an online "paper mill" and handing it in as one's own. DI students usually have no trouble understanding the seriousness of such offenses, and honor codes and clearly stated consequences are most often as effective a deterrent for them as for any other student.

However, the issue of plagiarism (another key component of academic integrity) is not so clear-cut and often leads to "honest confusion by the students, and disagreements among faculty" (Shi, 2004, p. 172). Standards for citations and paraphrasing can differ among subject areas and even among individual teachers. Some students worry that they will unknowingly commit plagiarism, as they are unsure of how or what to cite and unsure where the author's ideas end and theirs begin (Ashworth & Bannister, 1997). In high school and college, many students are not directly taught academic writing conventions for working with sources. In fact, college instructors, uncomfortable with discussing issues of possible plagiarism, often respond to student questions "indirectly" (Hyland, 2001), leaving students with no increased understanding of academic citation expectations or strategies to correct inadvertent instances of plagiarism in their papers. Furthermore, Ashworth and Bannister have found that college students admit "widespread ignorance" of citation and referencing rules, "even midway through their degree courses" (1997, p. 197). Clearly, academic source citation and integration must be more explicitly taught in college.

For most DI students, the issue of plagiarism is not necessarily one of academic dishonesty (as it is stated in the Penn State University policy), nor is it necessarily a lack of understanding the conventions of academic integrity (though this is often the case) once they are taught them, but rather it is an issue that highlights the need for advanced academic reading, writing, vocabulary, and grammatical skills that they do not yet possess. Many argue that student *patchwriting,* in which students only slightly alter the vocabulary and sentence structure of the original source and do not place original words in quotations, can be viewed as a developmental stage (Ouellette, 2008; Pecorari, 2003; Howard, 1995), which teachers should expect and "treat as an important transitional strategy" (Howard, 1995, p. 788), rather than as a "problem" (ibid.). In addition, many researchers and educators note that Generation 1.5 students and other ESL students plagiarize because of "poor time management and planning skills" (Harris, 2002, as cited in Lackie & D'Angelo-Long, 2004, p. 36) or "heavy workloads" (Pennycook, 1996) that do not allow students to put adequate time into the complex tasks needed when writing with sources. DI students must spend much more time on these tasks because they don't have the breadth of vocabulary to rephrase and may find the time demands overwhelming.

Instructors of DI students need to recognize the challenging reading, vocabulary, grammar, writing, and higher-level thinking demands of working and writing with sources and should provide adequate time, instruction, and hands-on practice to enable these students to be successful. Writing with sources should be viewed by DI students and instructors as a set of developing skills that can improve with incremental assignments and opportunities to respond to source text readings that enable them to practice the higher-level thinking skills of paraphrase, summary, and analysis.

Because basic writing and first-year composition courses traditionally demand less work with sources than college-level courses in other subject areas (Leki & Carson, 1997), it is critical that DI students are able to explore working and writing with sources in linked content courses and reading skills courses as well as in the composition classroom. A positive approach that emphasizes the learning process (rather than a punitive one that emphasizes catching student plagiarism) is one that allows DI students to grow in skills, confidence, and writing ability.

Goal 1: Teach the Concept of Intellectual Property as an American Value and the Importance of Citing Sources

---

Do I need to cite this?

—first-year developmental immigrant student

Challenge

Students from other countries have difficulty attributing sources in U.S. academic papers because ownership of one's own ideas is a very Western concept. Pennycook notes that Chinese education emphasizes the memorization of text in order to internalize ideas; in writing, quotations from these texts are then not attributed to their sources or even marked as quotations, as it is assumed that every learned Chinese knows these are the words of the wise and not the author's own (1996). Sherman found that her Italian students' university expected verbatim, memorized responses on exams, and that students believed that "taking over [the author's] words was . . . necessary in order to cover the subject, and also a mark of respect for the originator" (1992, p. 191).

Suggested Approaches

Instructors should explicitly discuss and teach the concept of intellectual property and its place in American academic work.

■ **Explain the Western idea of "intellectual property."**

By helping students understand the concept of ownership of ideas, perhaps by linking it to the U.S. value of individualism, instructors can help DI students understand the reasoning behind citing sources.

■ **Be clear about the consequences of intentional plagiarism.**

D'Angelo-Long (2004) reports that high school students who view a writing assignment as "busywork" (p. 73) are more likely to intentionally plagiarize, thinking "why bother with so much effort" if the instructor isn't likely to read the finished piece. By showing students that they read, respond, and value students' academic work, instructors also make it clear to students that they will follow up on acts of plagiarism. By explaining the campus plagiarism policies and procedures, instructors make it less likely that students will intentionally plagiarize.

■ **Be clear about what kind of information needs to be cited.**

Facts that are not common knowledge, anecdotes, statistics, expert opinion, personal observation, survey results, and direct quotations all need to be cited in an academic paper. It is important that instructors discuss each of these categories and determine examples of each, and compare them with common knowledge (such as "George Washington was the first president of the United States") that does not need citation. A good rule to tell students is: "If it didn't come out of your own head, it needs to be cited."

■ **Provide hands-on practice in deciding what needs citation.**

Placing information on strips of paper, breaking students into groups, and asking each group to determine which strips' information needs citing (and why) can be a useful activity for DI students.

■ **Provide practice in determining where outside support is needed to strengthen an argument.**

Instructors and peers can tell writers orally or in writing where a statistic, expert opinion, or other outside information could strengthen an argument. Peer readers can make notations directly on drafts where they think there needs to be more outside support and suggest the type of support that would be best. The support planning sheet in Figure 5.1 can also help DI students decide what should be included that needs to be cited.

■ **Require multiple drafts.**

Students who know that faculty are invested in their papers and will read and respond meaningfully to them are much less likely to plagiarize (D'Angelo-Long, 2004). In addition, multiple drafts allow the instructor to see students' thought process and idea development, and to assist students with proper citation format.

FIGURE 5.1
Support Planning Sheet

Name _____

Support Planning Sheet for an Argumentative (Persuasive) Essay

NOTE: Not ALL parts of this chart need to be filled out! The places where you need outside sources may vary according to your topic. In general, it's a good idea to have at least one outside source for most sections.

Section of Essay	Supporting Evidence (anecdotes, statistics, facts, expert opinion, survey results) *IMPORTANT: Be sure to put exact words in quotation marks or paraphrase significantly!*	Source (author + title + publication information)
Introduction/ Problem Statement		
First main point		
Second main point		
Third main point		

FIGURE 5.1 (Continued)
Support Planning Sheet

Section of Essay	Supporting Evidence (anecdotes, statistics, facts, expert opinion, survey results) IMPORTANT: Be sure to put exact words in quotation marks or paraphrase significantly!	Source (author + title + publication information)
Counterarguments		
Refutation of Counterarguments		
Conclusion		

Figure 5.1 is reproducible. Copyright © 2011 University of Michigan.

■ **Require that students hand in photocopies, printouts, or complete web addresses of their sources with their papers.**

If students know instructors will be referencing the original sources, students are usually much more careful to cite correctly and completely and to ask questions if they are unsure of how or whether to cite something.

Goal 2: Provide Clear Practice in Identifying Plagiarism, and Provide Direct Instruction and Hands-On Practice in Integrating Quotations, Paraphrasing, and Summarizing

---

I don't know if I'm plagiarizing.

Why do I need to change the way the author said it? He did a good job.

—first-year developmental immigrant students

Challenge

Students are often thrust into a research paper without having practiced integrating quotations, paraphrasing, and summarizing, which are all complex skills that require a sophisticated command of language. They are often overwhelmed with all the skills they must build, as very often teachers assume students have these skills or have picked them up along the way. However, just as students cannot learn a grammar rule and immediately transfer it to their own writing error-free (see Chapter 9), DI students cannot simply be told the rules of citation and paraphrase and be expected to produce correctly cited work immediately. Students will need to edit their own writing for proper citation, and hands-on practice in identifying plagiarism in the writing of others is a good first step in being able to identify plagiarism in their own writing.

Suggested Approaches

Because these skills are complex and require strong language skills, students need repeated hands-on practice and immediate feedback and meaning negotiation. Most online and textbook treatments of the topic of citing sources are prescriptive, rather than interactive. Hands-on, interactive experience working with texts will teach these concepts much better than assigning readings on the topic. Many of these activities can be integrated into a reading, writing, or content-area course, with or without a larger research paper as the goal.

■ **Use clear online plagiarism identification exercises as whole class, small group, and individual practice.**

In her analysis of ten North American college websites, Kyoto Yamada notes that most sample paraphrases on college writing websites "seem to have been written with such elaboration that at first glance inexperienced writers may not realize how they were generated" (2003, p. 250). However, DI students would benefit most from paraphrasing examples that are most accessible (Stolarek, 1994, as cited in Yamada 2003). Activities that involve students' determining if a sample paraphrase is correct or incorrect when compared with the source text are often more useful and engaging than simply having students read sample paraphrases without analyzing or judging them.

■ **Provide explicit instruction and practice in integrating quotations.**

Students need to understand that quotations must be introduced with signal phrases and interpreted or related in the sentence that follows them. They should understand that papers should have no *floating* quotations, quotations simply stuck into the paragraph with no connection or interpretation.

■ **Use summary writing as a tool for determining comprehension.**

Hoye (1988) found that college freshmen who received instruction and practice in summary writing earned higher reading comprehension scores than students who did not. Summary writing is an essential tool that can both increase and measure comprehension. However, many instructors avoid teaching it directly, as the skill is complex to both learn and teach.

Kissner asserts that in good summaries, the authors "include import ideas," "delete trivia," "delete repeated ideas," "collapse lists," and "choose or create a topic sentence" (2006, p. 10). Each of these skills must be taught explicitly and practiced. We have found that Kissner's book *Summarizing, Paraphrasing, and Retelling: Skills for Better Reading, Writing and Test-Taking* (2006), as well as many websites, are good resources on the topic.

Summarizing can also improve students' comprehension of lectures. Davis and Hult (1997) found that college students who wrote brief summaries of a lecture during 4-minute lecture breaks showed significant improvement in understanding. Asking students to summarize a lecture verbally (during a quick break in the lecture) or in writing (after the lecture or after a segment of it) can also help students' comprehension and allow instructors to assess comprehension.

Goal 3: Provide a Variety of Opportunities for Students to Practice Skills in Reading and Writing with Sources That Aren't Necessarily Full-Fledged Research Papers

The thought of a research paper stresses me out.

—first-year developmental immigrant student

Challenge

Instructors of DI students in both English and the content areas often assign a large research paper, usually at the end of the term, so that students can have the experience of writing with sources. Unfortunately, this can cause instructors and students to become frustrated, as students find that there is not enough time at the end of the term (particularly if more than one instructor assigns a large research paper) to learn and use the skills they need to complete the assignment successfully.

Suggested Approaches

It is essential that DI students gain experience working with sources. However, because of the skill demand and the need for students to develop this skill over time, instructors should provide frequent, more manageable experiences in working with sources and using higher-level thinking skills to analyze and respond to source texts.

■ **Provide frequent opportunities to orally paraphrase and summarize readings in class.**

Paraphrasing and summarizing are complex skills that are deeply linked to understanding text. By having students paraphrase or summarize readings orally or in writing, instructors can measure and deepen comprehension and provide much-needed practice in these higher-level skills. Instructors can read a short textbook excerpt, newspaper article, or even short story, and ask students to write down the most important ideas, after listening or taking notes while listening (putting exact words in quotations), and create a summary from that. Students can then work in groups to evaluate and refine their summaries. Students could also orally express the most important ideas as the instructor writes them on the board.

■ **Create an atmosphere of frequent class discussion and debate.**

Oral classroom arguments and discussions, in which students' positions are backed up by support from class readings, can deepen understanding of and connections between readings, strengthen argumentative skills, and provide practice in working with sources. Formal debate and informal discussion can be used to help students develop their thinking and support before writing an argumentative essay.

■ **Provide opportunities to respond to single readings in an analytical way.**

Working with multiple sources requires a level of synthesis that most writers (even very strong ones) find highly challenging. By focusing students on one text, instructors can provide practice in referencing and responding to sources without overwhelming students.

■ **Require students to support their argumentative essays with integrated direct quotations from three different sources.**

Because paraphrasing is so challenging, it can be beneficial to have students work with direct quotations only, before teaching them to integrate paraphrases as well. Limiting students to three sources can also make this activity less overwhelming and allow them to focus on necessary skills.

■ **Provide students with the opportunity to analyze a writer's argument.**

Asking students to analyze an argument requires them to work with a text in a critical way. This is a critical skill that requires students to think about the author's authority, purpose, position, claims, and support. This analysis can be done in class discussion, with students using excerpts of the text for support, and in writing, using a checklist of key questions as a starting point. Many good checklists are available online, including one from the University of Iowa Writing Center (www. uiowa.edu/~writingc): click on "Resources for Writers" and then "Writing about Controversies").

■ **Provide the opportunity for students to work in small groups on a PowerPoint, prezi.com, or poster presentation.**

By requiring students to analyze a theme in a reading or movie and then presenting this analysis in an oral and visual group presentation, instructors can help students focus on collaborative thinking skills. Students must correctly attribute direct quotations and use specific excerpts for support, yet do not need to focus on detailed MLA or APA rules in order to be successful.

Goal 4: Provide Guidance and Choices in Topic Selection, and Make the Process Manageable for Students When Assigning a Research Paper or Argumentative Essay

---

I couldn't find any sources for my side of the argument, so I decided to argue the other side.

—first-year developmental immigrant student

Challenge

DI students often become overwhelmed when faced with an assignment that involves reading and writing from sources. Because the assignment will likely be more time-consuming for them than for native speakers or stronger writers, and because DI students often have many responsibilities outside of school that take up much of their time, they may "give up" if they don't believe they will be successful. Many are also overwhelmed by choosing a topic, narrowing it, and sorting through online sources.

Suggested Approaches

Henry notes that "the greatest insurance against plagiarism [is] . . . the actual enjoyment and ownership of ideas" (2004, p. 83). By working with students to discover topics of interest to them, teaching students to break down assignments into manageable steps, and providing feedback at each writing stage, instructors can help to lessen anxiety and better ensure success and progress.

■ **Break the assignment into manageable steps.**

By dividing the assignment into distinct steps (each with its own due date) and providing explicit feedback at each stage, instructors can help students be less overwhelmed and more successful.

■ **Be certain students have adequate background knowledge in the topic if possible.**

By reading an argumentative essay on each side of a controversial issue, students gain background knowledge, can judge their own interest in the topic, and can further explore debates begun in class by doing additional research.

■ **Be certain students have topic choices and sufficient interest in the topic if possible.**

By providing a list of topic choices that relate to class topics and course readings, instructors can give students a starting point for topic choice. Students can also be encouraged to come up with their own topics and have them approved by the instructor. It can be helpful for students to hear what others are writing about; by listing topics on the board that everyone has chosen, students can find others to discuss a chosen topic with or gain ideas for their own topics. Instructor and students can also brainstorm topic ideas as a whole class or in small groups.

■ **Help students narrow and refine their topics.**

This may involve informal individual conferencing, brainstorming activities, assistance from campus librarians, or discussion with tutors in the learning center.

■ **Utilize the campus learning center or tutors to provide more one-on-one feedback and reading support.**

The immediate feedback of working with a tutor and the ability to discuss the meaning of readings can help DI students navigate the writing and reading assignment more successfully.

■ **Help students use technology to their advantage.**

Many online tools exist for student researchers. Sites such as easybib.com ask students for specific bibliographic information and then format the Works Cited page automatically. Sites like bibme.org even fill in bibliographic information for many entries if students enter an author's name and article title: the site then creates a correctly formatted Works Cited page. Many of these sites allow students to save their source information and add to it as they work.

A library visit during class time can allow campus librarians to teach students how to use the campus library's online search engine and reference materials. They can also provide instruction in evaluating online sources. Such instruction is also usually found on the campus library homepage.

Writing with sources requires a complex skill set that many developmental immigrant students do not yet possess. By working with students along a continuum of activities and assignments that provide adequate time, explicit practice, and explicit feedback, instructors in a variety of first-year classes can help DI students develop into more confident academic writers.

Additional Useful Websites

- **Exercise Central**
  www.bedfordstmartins.com/exercisecentral
  Contains exercises on identifying common knowledge. Click on the exercises tab, and then click on Comprehensive Study Plan to find Writing with Sources and then Recognizing Common Knowledge.

- **Diana Hacker's *A Writer's Reference* Website**
  http://bcs.bedfordstmartins.com/writersref6e
  Click on Research Exercises for many good exercises on working with and integrating sources. Click on ESL Help for the useful chart Integrating and citing sources to avoid plagiarism.

- **David Gardner's "Plagiarism and How to Avoid It"**
  http://www.ec.hku.hk/plagiarism/
  Helps students identify different levels of plagiarism.

- **The Writing Center at Syracuse University**
  wrt.syr.edu/670/downloads/205heuristics/205-Sourcing/IntegratingQuotations.doc
  Useful handout on integrating quotations. Provides examples, a list of signal words, and examples of acceptable and unacceptable levels of integration.

- **Raymond Jones' ReadingQuest**
  www.readingquest.org/strat/summarize.html
  Offers many activities and suggestions for teaching summary writing.

- **Noodletools**
  www.noodletools.com
  Contains links to bibliography tools and useful search engines for research.

- **Clusty**
  www.clusty.com/
  Useful search engine for research papers.

- **O'Keefe Library's "Best Information on the Net"**
  library.sau.edu/bestinfo/Hot/hotindex.htm

- **Multnomah County Library Homework Center Social Issues page**
  www.multcolib.org/homework/sochc.html
  Starting points for researching many controversial issues.

- **The Library Information Index**
  www.lii.org
  Provides relevant, useful sources that have been reviewed by librarians.

Chapter 6

Teaching a Content-Based Course: American Studies

KEY POINTS

- ☞ Content-based instruction enables students to acquire academic literacy through a combination of academic and language instruction.

- ☞ In a content-based course, developmental immigrant students learn technical vocabulary, background knowledge, and higher-order thinking skills.

I always knew that Americans had a history, but I never knew that they had any culture. . . .

—*first-year developmental immigrant student*

Much has been written about the benefits of academic instruction through content-based courses (Benesch, 1988; Kasper, 1994, 1997; Heller & Greenleaf, 2007; Brown, Park, Jeong, & Staples, 2006; Pohan & Kelly, 2004; Chamot, 2004). This research has shown that content-based courses teach immigrant students the academic literacy necessary for success in mainstream college courses by expanding their knowledge base (Kasper, 1998) and increasing their English language proficiency. In other words, academic literacy is a combination of academic instruction and language instruction. Cummins (1981) distinguishes between social (conversational) or basic interpersonal communicative skills (BICS), which usually take two to three years to acquire, and academic English or cognitive academic language proficiency (CALP), which usually requires five to seven years, and that, for many DI students, continues to evolve in college. Both are important, but in order for students to be successful in their undergraduate coursework and in their professional fields, it is necessary for them to understand the difference between the two types of skills and to learn the content-specific language in their humanities, science, and social science classes. Content-specific language involves learning technical vocabulary (Chamot & O'Malley, 1994) and background knowledge (Brown, 2004), which will result in higher-order thinking and problem-solving skills (Brown, 2004).

The National Research Council (NRC, 1999) found that in order for students to succeed in college they need instruction to gain: (1) in-depth knowledge of content and subject matter, (2) conceptual understanding to gain awareness of knowledge structures in each discipline, and (3) critical-thinking skills to be able to learn, think, and solve problems within the discipline. Faculty can help DI students gain these insights through multiple examples and practical application of concepts to real-life issues, and by connecting new knowledge to prior knowledge (NRC, 1999).

In alignment with the NRC's call to strengthen student learning through content-based courses, the "hub" course in Penn State Brandywine's American Studies Cluster is content-based. American Studies approaches the study of U.S. history and American culture by looking at what is familiar to the students in the present and tracing their origins, offering students the reading, vocabulary, and background knowledge needed to understand American history and culture. The thematic units in the course drive the writing, grammar, and reading classes, which further develop and nurture the academic literacies and competencies of these students. For example, most of our developmental immigrant students are familiar with the proliferation of guns and violence in America (most live in inner-city Philadelphia). What they are not familiar with, however, is the fact that guns are part of early history, the early frontiers (the Wild West and pioneering spirit), and are a fundamental right (included in the Second Amendment).

By building on the academic reading and literacy tasks in the American Studies course, faculty in the other cluster courses are able to reinforce concepts taught and lessons learned, and students begin to realize that the courses they take in college are interconnected and dynamic rather than disconnected and discrete. Students also get a sense of the American experience: who Americans are as a nation and as a people, from both multicultural and interdisciplinary perspectives, enriching the overall classroom experience. In this way, the classroom becomes a collaborative, inquiry-oriented learning environment, which fosters student engagement in worthy discipline-based discourse (Heller & Greenleaf, 2007).

Goal 1: Recognize and Address the Specialized Use of Language across Disciplines

---

Sometimes I don't get the technical words the teacher uses.

—first-year developmental immigrant student

Challenge

Because every discipline has its own way of communicating information, every academic subject presents students with distinct challenges. Students need to be provided with the opportunity to learn discipline-based knowledge, concepts, and vocabulary to increase their capacity to read and understand a broader range of texts in college (Heller & Greenleaf, 2007).

Suggested Approaches

Content-based courses have a dual focus: they teach language and subject matter simultaneously, with course content guiding language presentation (Kasper, 2000). Therefore, faculty should address the specialized use of language across and within disciplines by teaching different ways of thinking, reading, writing, and speaking in each of them. This can include specific purposes for reading and writing, for tests and for knowledge, as well as valued reasoning processes such as arguing, questioning, and analyzing evidence, problems, and solutions. Discipline-based faculty can present ideas through charts, tables, illustrations, and different text types (Heller & Greenleaf, 2007).

Each of these literacies needs to be taught, along with the content-related material, so that students can compete academically in higher education. Teaching content-based strategies within a content-based course is a logical and appropriate way to do this.

■ **Provide students with the opportunity to learn content information, concepts, and vocabulary to broaden their capacity to read and understand a broader range of texts through thematic units.**

This information can come from a variety of sources, including textbooks, scholarly articles, news magazines (*Time* or *Newsweek*, for example), or online sources. Extensive reading on a topic gives students a chance to read more challenging material.

For example, in the American Studies course, when students study the Civil Rights movement, they read textbooks and a variety of magazine and journal articles on the movement (and its history). They read about the people associated with this movement so that they can better understand why affirmative action, Martin Luther King Jr. Day, quotas, and other (somewhat) familiar concepts are now laws and/ or are continually being debated within the U.S. legislative and judicial systems. The vocabulary found in each of these sources varies, so it is helpful to discuss the differences and similarities in both language use and purpose among the various reading material.

■ **Provide students with the opportunity to engage in class discussions.**

Class discussions can provide students with the opportunity to talk about their own experiences on a particular topic, such as their own experiences with discrimination. Instructors can then compare and/or contrast the students' experiences with the material being presented (the Civil Rights movement, for example). These discussions also reinforce the reading material, making it more comprehensible for the students. Comprehensible input also leads to increased language proficiency, including the vocabulary and grammar of the language, according to Krashen (1985).

■ **Teach the complexities associated with a content-based course.**

In the American Studies course "the American way of life" is often discussed, but for many DI students, it is not an easy phenomenon to explain. To better understand the complexities that underlie the American culture, DI students read books (their texts and other course-related books) as well as scholarly articles within each unit; they see films (such as *Eye on the Prize,* for a wonderful overview of the Civil Rights movement); and they engage in class discussions and debates to learn about the history. Because the complexities require that students go beyond simply reading texts and writing essays, they engage in higher-order thinking skills as they read and write, analyzing and responding to the readings for class discussions and tests.

For example, in the unit on Government and Politics, students learn about the voting process. In election years, they do research on the candidates, write about each candidate's platform, and determine who the *instructor* should vote for, and why (students are very careful in this assignment because it involves the instructor rather than friends or themselves). Students are also provided with voting forms so that they can register to vote if they are legally able to. They also learn about the Electoral College and debate its advantages and disadvantages. In other words, rich and challenging content learning, in addition to strategic instructional support (Heller & Greenleaf, 2007), helps DI students increase their content-based foundational knowledge.

Goal 2: Bridge Immigrant Communities and Mainstream American Society

My daily life is lived in the American culture, and as hard as I may fight it, the Vietnamese culture still exists in my home . . . am I American or am I Vietnamese? I'm technically American but was raised Vietnamese; it's very confusing for me.

At home I am a Liberian; at school I am a Liberian who behaves like an American.

Why can't Americans understand that I'm not African-American or African, I'm Haitian. It's so confusing.

—first-year developmental immigrant students

Challenge

Many DI students aren't sure who they are. They don't understand that they are part of the United States' bigger immigration story. Also, because they move along a cultural continuum, depending on the context, they sometimes don't see their bicultural identity as something positive, but rather as something negative or confusing, at the very least. In other words, most are becoming independent of their family or country of origin at the same time that they are coming to terms with which culture they should belong to, causing them to feel culturally conflicted at times. On the one hand, they want to fit into the American culture; on the other hand, to do so means that in some ways they are turning away from their families, the very people that have enabled them to go to college.

Suggested Approaches

Provide ways to help students recognize and acknowledge their complexity so that they can gain control of themselves as individuals living between two cultures. They need to understand that they *are* the American experience and that their biculturalism should be viewed as a strength.

■ **Define the American experience for students.**

Instructors can discuss with students the immigration patterns to the United States, especially the four major waves of immigration: from 1815 to the 1840s (primarily Irish, Germans, and English); post–Civil War, 1860s to the 1880s (primarily Germans, Scandinavians, and English); the 1880s to World War I (primarily eastern European Jews, Russians, Poles, Ukrainians, Lithuanians, Italians, Greeks, and others from this part of the world); and 1965 to the present (primarily Europe, Mexico, Philippines, Jamaica, El Salvador, Haiti, Vietnam, Korea, India, China, Liberia, Nigeria, and other African nations).

Part of this discussion can include looking at websites where students can trace how the immigration patterns have changed (see Useful Websites at end of chapter).

■ Encourage students to participate in campus activities, especially multicultural events.

Students who get involved in multicultural events on campus meet many more students and faculty members. They also are able to share and showcase their own cultures so that "traditional" students can broaden their knowledge about world cultures and peoples. For example, at Penn State Brandywine, the multicultural students have their own club and hold a multicultural dinner/fashion show event, which is one of the best attended events on campus. Our immigrant students are so proud of this event as it truly bridges cultures and people.

■ Provide opportunities for students to reflect on being bicultural in the U.S.

When students have in-class opportunities to verbalize their thoughts and feelings on being bicultural, they realize that they share similar fears and anxieties. All students may not want to talk about this in public; therefore, instructors should not force them. Once the class has shared stories and experiences, barriers tend to be removed. For example, during a discussion in the American Studies class, one student stated that she began to recognize that who she is often depends on where she is. This Taiwanese student commented, "Even though I am Taiwanese, at school I must *act* American." This type of revelation suggests that for this particular group of students, their complexity is not just about language. It is also about culture at both the conscious and subconscious levels and about understanding appropriate behaviors and expectations in both cultures. DI students need to know that they undergo a process of negotiation and re-negotiation in terms of their identity as they navigate between the two cultural systems. After the discussions, students can reflect through a written narrative on their personal experience.

■ Set up a student partnering program.

Leki (2001) states that more significant than classrooms and teachers are the academic relationships that second language learners form with traditional students. Partnering traditional students with DI students is positive for both the students and the Penn State Brandywine campus community. For example, education majors and immigrant students organized and participated in a joint seminar: the immigrant students spoke about their educational experiences, both in their native countries and in the United States, and the education majors asked questions regarding these experiences. The education majors were amazed by the DI students' educational experiences, which led to an animated discussion between both groups that continued after the seminar was over.

■ **Invite multicultural speakers who can talk about their own experiences and serve as role models for the students.**

Cathy Bao Bean visited Penn State Brandywine, for example, and talked about her "Chopsticks-Fork Principle" (knowing when and how to use chopsticks and when and how to use forks as a metaphor for negotiating two cultures) and her "Duck-Rabbit Principle" (how, in "trick" drawings, a person can see a duck or a rabbit, but never both at the same time, just like people can operate in one culture or the other but not both simultaneously). Her presentation resonated strongly with our students.

Goal 3: Introduce Students to the Higher Education System: First-Year Seminar

---

College seems so strange like a magic life.

—*first-year developmental immigrant student*

Challenge

First-Year Seminar (FYS), also referred to as First-Year Engagement, First-Year Experience, or other similar names, has become a part of many undergraduate programs throughout the United States. FYS, which may or may not be attached to a content course, is designed to provide first-year university students with the skills they need for academic survival. The focus of FYS is to develop and improve communication, research, and critical-thinking and computer literacy skills. Two FYS goals at Penn State Brandywine are:

❑ To engage students in learning and orient them to the scholarly community from the outset of their undergraduate studies in a way that will bridge to later experiences in their chosen majors

❑ To facilitate students' adjustment to the high expectations, demanding workload, increased liberties, and other aspects of the transition to college life

The problem for DI students, however, is that their special needs are usually not addressed or even recognized in many FYS courses. Just how do faculty "facilitate students' adjustment to the high expectations and demanding workload" when a large proportion of these students come from different cultural and academic traditions and contexts? The problem becomes exacerbated by the fact that many DI students are part of the 70 percent of high school graduates who are not proficient readers and who are not college ready (Greene & Forster, 2003). In some ways, the larger issue is that some FYS instructors do not recognize DI student needs.

Suggested Approaches

Instructors should be sensitive to the fact that DI students may have had a variety of educational experiences, which could make the transition to college more problematic for them. Discipline-based instructors should also use the first-year seminar as the course in which to identify those students who might need extra academic support than what is ordinarily taught in a FYS course, whether it be in the form of outside help (such as learning center support staff or ESL faculty support) or in the form of additional emphasis on academic expectations and requirements (in FYS). If possible, FYS should be linked with a content-based course taught exclusively to DI students for greater impact and focus (at Penn State Brandywine it is linked with American Studies).

■ **Organize FYS sessions as a group discussion.**

When DI students participate in (or at least listen to) discussions, they learn from them. For example, in the American Studies class, the FYS discussions center on campus-related topics, which are usually "non-issues" for traditional students, such as the cultural similarities and differences related to a particular topic (such as how to address professors). Group discussions allow students to share their thoughts on a topic more in depth, to recognize differences in how instructors present information, and to discuss appropriate ways of responding and participating in class.

■ **Organize a seminar series.**

The FYS component of the American Studies course launched a faculty seminar series (related to the various units in the American Studies course), where faculty across disciplines come in and give a lecture to the students in their areas of expertise. The purpose of these lectures is to provide the students with a more in-depth perspective of a particular academic discipline and its relationship to American culture, to familiarize DI students with other faculty and courses on campus (this also helps students become more comfortable with other faculty on campus), and to familiarize faculty with this population of students. For example, during the unit on religion in the U.S., the Religious Studies professor spoke to the students about various Protestant denominations. When the professor asked how many of the students

had been to a Protestant church, not one hand went up; he was shocked and realized that he needed to rethink and re-address his assumptions when lecturing to
students. Though the faculty members have had immigrant students in their classes
(and have had varying experiences associated with these students), they have never
taught a class of *only* immigrant students, where the students are not afraid to
respond to and ask questions, where they engage in meaningful and enthusiastic
discussion, where they approach discussions from a wide range of multicultural
perspectives, and where they exude a confidence and competence not often found
in their mainstream classes.

- **Incorporate technology into lessons.**

Inherent within the goals or objectives of the FYS is gaining literacy in computer
use for academic purposes (doing research, PowerPoint presentations, etc.). Faculty
can assign topics related to content material in the course and ask the students, in
groups, to prepare a PowerPoint presentation (which will also improve their public
speaking skills) on a particular topic. Group work fosters team effort; it is also a
pedagogical strategy used in many college courses.

Goal 4: Provide an Opportunity for Students to Engage in Undergraduate Research and Leadership Opportunities (in Institutions Where Research Opportunities Are Available to Undergraduate Students)

I can't believe how much I learned at the conference. The students were
from all over the country and they were so nice. I made some great friends.

—former developmental immigrant student

Challenge

DI students are often unaware of research, publication, and leadership opportunities available to them on and off college campuses throughout their academic careers.
With encouragement from faculty, these students can take risks and reap benefits in
ways that they never thought were possible.

Suggested Approaches

Faculty should seek opportunities for DI students to share their global literacies with both the campus community and the wider community.

- **Immigrant students are in a unique position to share a wide variety of cultural traditions.**

DI students can greatly benefit from undergraduate research in ways that the literature hasn't addressed: it gives students a strong sense of identity, scholarship, and collegiality. One way of engaging students in undergraduate research is through campus-wide exhibitions by undergraduate students. For example, four of our immigrant students received funding to do research on their native cultural wedding traditions, which they shared along with photographic records of these traditions, during a research symposium on our campus (in fact, their research grants launched a student-faculty wedding tradition exhibition, involving the entire campus). This symposium fostered pride in as well as recognition of the diverse contributions and the many traditions, which make up the American experience on the college campus.

- **Encourage students to submit their writing (either essays or poetry/short stories) or artwork to campus or other college writing journals.**

Several DI students at Penn State Brandywine have had their essays published in universitywide writing journals. Others have submitted their creative writing (poems and short stories) or artistic creations to on-campus publications. In addition, recently, all of our first-year DI students had one of their essays (self-chosen) published in an in-house journal. Many DI students have "hidden talents" that have not been showcased. Being published is an enormous source of pride and accomplishment. Getting an essay published enables DI students to view themselves as being able to write in English.

- **Encourage students to participate in undergraduate research at the local, state, national, or international level.**

Students can go through the process of submitting abstracts, writing articles, and presenting their research at professional meetings, all of which contribute to the building of knowledge structures. They can compete with students from all over the country and get to know students from around the world at these meetings. Students will naturally feel good about themselves and about representing their college, and these meetings can also provide valuable contacts for future research, academic, or job opportunities.

- **Encourage students to take on leadership roles on campus.**

DI students are often not aware of how to go about running for student government office or how to become a student leader on campus. Sometimes taking a moment to mention leadership opportunities in class can make all the difference in students' decisions to apply for them. With encouragement from the faculty, these students not only can become leaders on campus (boosting their self-esteem), but they can also serve as role models for other international students. For example, several of our students have served as orientation leaders for incoming first-year students and several have run for student government positions—and won! DI students not only feel more confident about their leadership abilities, but they also become a vital part of the campus academic community.

Content-based instruction helps developmental immigrant students improve their English language proficiency through the medium of a discipline-specific course. Though language instruction can be integrated into any subject matter, it works particularly well in a course like American Studies, where students are exposed to discipline-based knowledge (and the language associated with it), learn important concepts about U.S. history and culture, and better understand their new country and the system of higher education within it.

Useful Websites for American Studies and U.S. History Courses

- **The New York Times' Immigration Explorer**
  http://www.nytimes.com/interactive/2009/03/10/us/20090310-immigration-explorer.html
  Interactive website where students can drag the arrow along the timeline and see how the immigration patterns in the United States have changed.

- **The History Channel**
  www.history.com
  Many video clips and educational materials.

Chapter 7

Teaching Reading

KEY POINTS

☞ Developmental immigrant students can improve their academic reading and critical thinking skills by working with authentic texts, learning and applying specific reading skills to these texts, and making reading-writing connections.

☞ In order for developmental immigrant students to become better readers, instructors should view them as full participants in the academic classroom community from the very beginning of the semester.

I never read a whole book before.

I hate reading. It takes too long.

—first-year developmental immigrant students

When developmental immigrant students first enter college, they usually believe that they will not have a problem handling college reading demands. They earned high grades in their high school classes, but they do not realize that these courses, for the most part, did not require the critical thinking and reasoning that college courses typically require. Many studies suggest that students who are "ethnically or socioeconomically outside the mainstream" (Greenleaf et al., 2001, p. 85) receive more basic-skills instruction than "mainstream" students, who are more often given higher-level thinking tasks (Allinton, 1991; Darling-Hammond, 1995; Levin, 1997; all as cited in Greenleaf et al., 2001). In fact, many DI students are placed in lower-track courses in high school (Forrest, 2006). Allison (2009) observes that in many high school basic social studies and science classes, teachers use PowerPoint slides to deliver key points from the textbooks. Students are then required to use the PowerPoint, which contains "predominately brief, decontextualized phrases" (p. 79) to complete worksheets, which emphasize "knowledge identification," rather than "application, analysis, or evaluation" (Allison, 2009). Students do not read the textbooks, other than to look up a specific answer they cannot find in their notes.

In college, however, students must read large volumes of text and are expected to apply higher-level thinking skills. Shih notes that:

> In academic content classes, students must not only comprehend texts, but over the long term, critically react to the content (e.g., in class discussion some time after reading an assignment), recall main points and details when tested (perhaps several weeks after initial reading), and synthesize information from reading with other related information, such as from lectures, discussion, and critical thinking (1992, p. 290).

This academic "jump" is difficult for most students transitioning to college but is even more pronounced for DI students, who do not have the skills in academic English to handle the vocabulary and syntax of college-level reading. In fact, many DI students enter college reading at the eighth- or ninth-grade level (Goldschmidt & Ziemba, 2003). They lack necessary background knowledge, have few reading strategies, and may not even be fluent readers in their native languages (Goldschmidt & Ziemba, 2003). They also may have had interrupted schooling in their native countries, putting them even further behind.

One common remedial approach for such students is a traditional developmental reading course that many times focuses on target skills in isolation through workbook exercises and short reading excerpts. However, such an approach simply puts DI students further behind (Maloney, 2003), as it does not allow them to work with authentic college texts and move from "learning to read" to "reading to learn" (Shih, 1992, p. 290; Greenleaf et al., 2001, p. 82). Allen (2000) and Greenleaf et al. (2001) observe that students need to be viewed as "Reading Apprentices" (a term coined by Schoenbach et al., 1999) whose teachers model the thinking skills needed for reading. Students and teachers then become a community of readers who read, think, and talk about their readings together.

Maloney asserts that "if at-risk college students are held to high standards, directly taught strategies for accomplishing good work within academic conventions, informed of the demands of the institution, and treated as colleagues in the shared adventure of learning, they can participate fully and successfully in the intellectual life of the college" (2003, p. 664). Instead of viewing students from a deficiency model (Davies, Safarik, & Banning, 2003), instructors should see developmental students as full participants in the academic classroom community from the very beginning. It is key that students work with authentic college texts, that teachers model reading and thinking skills (Shih, 1992), and that students are given ample time and practice to acquire these strategies so that they can think, respond, and question as a community of learners.

The goals and activities described in this chapter can be used in content courses across the curriculum, in stand-alone English for Academic Purposes reading courses, or in reading courses linked to a content course. Kasper has found that a reading course paired with a psychology course leads to a higher pass rate in the psychology course (1995), that reading courses "which are not paired, but based in an academic discipline" may also be beneficial to students (1995, p. 298), and that courses with readings from multiple disciplines can have academic benefits for students in the following semester (1997). Our campus' American Studies cluster has had success linking the Reading course with the American Studies course. Because both courses require the same textbooks, the reading teacher is able to reinforce, supplement, and deepen what is discussed in American Studies. Our second semester International Literature and Film course links reading, writing, and cinema in order to deepen students' analytical thinking and expression. No matter what the course is, any help with reading skills that instructors can provide will benefit DI students.

Reading is a complex skill set that must grow with the student. One reading course in one semester is not enough to build the academic and critical literacy of DI students to the level that they need for academic success. We strongly suggest a first semester reading course (content-based or linked to a content course) and a second semester reading-writing course, as well as ongoing support (through all four years of college) from the campus learning center.

Goal 1: Create a Clear Purpose and Motivation for Reading

I hate reading. It's hard.

Why do we have to read so much?

—first-year developmental students

Challenge

DI students, like many new college students, almost universally "hate" reading, finding it time-consuming and overwhelming. Most do not know how to apply reading strategies and are quickly overwhelmed by the sheer volume of reading in college.

Suggested Approaches

Instructors should acknowledge students' challenges and help them break down the overwhelming concept of "reading."

- **Allow students to assess their current reading strategies.**

Students enrolled in a reading course can take a survey to determine what strategies they currently use. One such survey is listed in Figure 7.1 on pages 91–92. A class discussion of survey results can emphasize that reading is a set of thinking skills and strategies that can be developed and learned. Used at the beginning of a course, the survey can help set course goals. (Students may need to have some survey terms defined for them.) At the end of a course, the survey can help students assess their progress and set future goals.

- **Survey students' current reading habits.**

Students in most courses can list the types of reading they already do so that they begin to see themselves as readers and can apply this knowledge to future reading as well. See Figure 7.2 on page 93.

- **Provide a clear purpose with every assignment.**

Students become motivated to read when they know why they are reading. The purpose may be to gain background knowledge, to obtain specific information, to practice a specific skill, or to answer a specific question. By knowing why they are reading, students can attempt to determine the best strategy for this type of reading and can begin to take control of their own learning.

- **Hold students accountable.**

For most students, reading is easy to fake. If they don't read an assignment, they can simply sit quietly in class, make general comments or react to another student's remark, or simply learn about the reading from listening to class discussion. Tovani (2000) notes that in middle school and high school, book reports are easy for students to fake, as they need only skim through the book and read its inside flaps to get all the information they need for those assignments. In college, it is essential that students be required to demonstrate their understanding of and thinking about what they read in a way that cannot be easily faked. One excellent way to do this is to require students to hand in a reading response to what they've read.

- **Provide accessible fiction for reading enjoyment.**

Most DI students have never read an entire book for enjoyment. Introducing a choice of adolescent fiction into the course syllabus can help students find enjoyable reads that are not overwhelming and can increase their motivation to read. One series that we have found effective is the First Person Fiction series (Orchard Books). Each of

FIGURE 7.1
Reading Strategy Survey

Name _____

A Measurement Instrument on the Use of Reading Strategies

DIRECTIONS: This instrument is designed to investigate your use of reading strategies in reading. In the next section, you will find a number of statements that describe how people read English. Please read each statement carefully. Next to each statement, write the response (1,2,3,4,5,6, or 7) that tells HOW TRUE OF YOU THE STATEMENT IS.

1. Never true of me
2. Almost never true of me
3. Usually not true of me
4. Somewhat true of me
5. Usually true of me
6. Almost always true of me
7. Always true of me

Answer in terms of how well the statement describes you. Do not answer how you think you should be or what other people do. There are no right or wrong answers to these statements. Read the following statements, and choose a response (1 through 7 as described above), and write it in the space provided after each statement.

1. I read English without looking up every new word in the dictionary.

2. I guess the meaning of a new word by looking at the words around it.

3. I pay more attention to the overall idea of a passage than the individual words in it.

4. I use prefixes and suffixes to guess the meaning of an unfamiliar word.

5. I use restatement to guess the meaning of a new word.

6. When I read a passage, I use what I already know about the topic to help me understand the information.

7. Before I read a passage, I use the background information provided by the teacher to actively predict the content of the passage.

8. When I read a passage, I get an overall idea about the content by looking at the structure (title, abstract, introduction, conclusion, and headings).

9. When I read a passage, I try to find the main idea and revise the main idea if necessary later on.

10. To understand a text, I pay more attention to topic sentences. (Sentences that contain main points of a paragraph. They are usually at the beginning of a paragraph.)

11. To understand a passage, I try to figure out what happens first, second, third, and so on.

12. To understand a passage, I look at similarities and differences between the events, objects, or people.

13. To understand a passage, I classify the information into categories or groups.

14. To understand a passage, I try to remember descriptions of people, places, events, objects, and so on.

15. To understand a passage, I analyze the problem posed by the author and the possible solutions.

16. To understand a passage, I look for causes and effects.

17. When I read a story, I visualize in my mind the people, the places, and the events of the story.

18. When I read a story, I try to understand how the people in the story feel by putting myself in the same situation.

19. When I take a reading test, I read the questions first and then look for the answers to the questions in the passage.

20. In dealing with multiple-choice questions, I eliminate unlikely answers first and then locate the right one.

From Zhang, 1994, pp. 23–25. Used with permission.

FIGURE 7.2
Reading Habits Survey

Name _____ Week of the Semester _____

Major _____ Native Language (if different from English) _____

Directions: Please record **all** the reading you do during the week in the space. Be sure to include the type of reading you do on that day, e.g., textbook reading, newspaper reading, email reading, etc. Also, include how much you read (e.g., how many pages) and/or the amount of time you spend reading (e.g., 15 minutes, 45 minutes, 90 minutes, etc.). It is assumed that the reading you record in this log is in English. If you are reading in your first language, please indicate that and provide the same information for the reading that you do in your first language as you do for the reading you do in English.

Monday

Tuesday

Wednesday

Thursday

Friday

Saturday

Sunday

Created by Cate Crosby, West Chester University. Used with permission.

the four novels tells the story of a teenager who immigrated to America (sometimes during the teen years, sometimes as a child). Students can discuss these books in literature circles, which are described in Goal 3 (see pg. 95).

■ **Introduce response journals.**

Response journals can be a powerful way for students to interact with and think about the text and take ownership of their reading. Typed submissions tend to be written more thoughtfully and revised more by students. Also, students who have written responses before class discussion are more engaged and critical during discussion. If two short readings are assigned, asking students to read both and choose one to respond to gives them some ownership over their reading and response.

Goal 2: Build Students' Background Knowledge

What is rice pudding?

Who was Jesus exactly?

—first-year developmental immigrant students

Challenge

DI students may struggle with reading simply because they lack the background knowledge needed to sufficiently comprehend a text. College-level texts introduce new information to students, but they also assume a certain knowledge base of their readers.

Suggested Approaches

By providing students with background knowledge, instructors create a knowledge base and context for reading.

■ **Provide several related readings that increase in difficulty to build background knowledge.**

Students can begin by reading newspapers and online articles related to a topic and then move on to reading trade journals and textbooks on the same topic as their knowledge base increases.

■ **Provide mini-lessons on necessary background knowledge before reading.**

Instructors should pull out essential cultural information from a reading and introduce this information before students read; these lessons can be brief. Students could also be assigned to research some of this information before a reading and share it with the class or in small groups, such as in a jigsaw, in which each student in a group is assigned a particular topic to research and teach to the group.

■ **Whenever possible, use visuals to build background knowledge.**

Technology makes it easy to bring background knowledge into the classroom. Pulling up a picture from the Internet or a short video clip from YouTube can bring historical and cultural information to life for students. Such illustrations can make key references clear. Relevant comic strips can also be used to teach culture and humor.

■ **Ask students to freewrite on what they already know about a topic.**

Before students begin a reading, instructors can introduce it by stating what the general theme, setting, or important idea of the reading is and then asking students to freewrite on what they already know about this topic. These responses can be shared in class discussion. Students can then more easily relate personal experience and background knowledge to the reading, and misconceptions can be cleared up before the text is read. Students can write again after they read, connecting what they discovered in the text with their earlier freewriting.

Goal 3: Build Students' Reading Comprehension by Teaching Specific Strategies within the Context of Authentic Readings

---

I want to understand better.

I read the words, but I don't know what it is saying.

—first-year developmental immigrant students

Challenge

Most DI students say that they would like to improve their reading comprehension. Many of them can read the words, but they have difficulty in grasping the deeper meaning.

Suggested Approaches

By encouraging students to actively engage with the text and modeling thinking strategies, instructors can help students improve comprehension.

■ **Model "talking to the text."**

Instructors can verbalize their own thought processes as they read a text out loud to students, thereby modeling the thinking skills and strategies active readers employ. Students can also practice talking to the text by writing their thoughts and questions in the margins of the text as they read. Schoenbach et al. (1999) is an excellent resource on this topic.

■ **Provide practice and instruction in making inferences.**

Students need to be shown that not everything in a text is directly stated. This is best done within the context of a class reading, but can be introduced and emphasized through exercises in a student text such as *Reader's Choice* (Silberstein, Clarke, & Dobson, 2008), which we have used at Penn State Brandywine.

■ **Teach text structure.**

When students understand how a text is organized, they can better understand the text itself. Students should become familiar with common rhetorical structures in English and with the organizational structures of college textbooks. Students can create concept maps or outlines to analyze the organization and important ideas of a text.

■ **Use literature circles.**

Literature circles can take many forms. Essentially, they are small student discussion groups in which each student is given a specific role and all work together to deepen their understanding of a text. Dillon (2007) found that developmental college readers who used literature circles improved their reading comprehension. Literature circles can be used with fiction or non-fiction, with books the groups choose from a teacher-generated list, or with a specific text assigned to the whole class.

■ **Ask students to write quick summaries.**

After students read a short passage in class, instructors can ask DI students to cover up the reading and write a quick summary of the text. Students can then compare their summaries in small groups and determine what should be added or deleted.

■ **Teach students to annotate text.**

Active readers write in the margins: summarizing, prioritizing, and restating in their own words.

■ **Use sticky notes to make connections.**

Keene and Zimmerman (1997) have observed that students comprehend better when they make several different kinds of connections: text-to-self, text-to-text, and text-to-world. Text-to-self connects the text to the reader's personal experience. Text-to-text connects one text to another text that may be similar in author, style, or theme. Text-to-world connects the reading to the reader's real-world knowledge or learning experiences (such as a current event or television program). To emphasize these connections, students can write each connection they make on a sticky-note. (The activity can be limited to one type of connection or even color-coded to distinguish the three types.) These sticky notes can be placed in the margins of the texts as a visual representation of students' thought processes and a prompt for class discussion.

■ **Ask students to write discussion questions about a reading on index cards to hand in at the beginning of class.**

Students are sometimes more apt to ask questions if they know they will be anonymous.

Goal 4: Build Students' Reading Fluency and Reading Speed

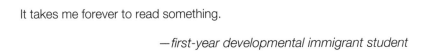

It takes me forever to read something.

—*first-year developmental immigrant student*

Challenge

Some DI students read slowly, word-by-word, particularly with academic texts. This sentence-level (or often, word-level) approach makes comprehension difficult, if not impossible, and the slow pace makes college reading loads overwhelming. Also, students whose native languages (such as Chinese) are not alphabet-based find reading English particularly laborious.

Suggested Approaches

Developmental immigrant students need practice in order to break the habit of reading everything word-by-word.

■ **Help students increase reading speed through timed readings.**

DI students often read slowly because they read word-by-word and sub-vocalize each word. Online speed reading lessons can help students break this habit. In addition, timed reading exercises, such as those found in several language textbooks, can help students increase their reading speed and comprehension. Grabe (2009), [citing Kuhn & Stahl (2003); National Reading Panel (2000); Samuels (2002); and

Segalowitz (2000)], asserts that "fluency, and especially automaticity, allows learners to attend to the meaning of the text, the textual context, and required background knowledge without being slowed down by attentional word recognition demands" (p. 291). Grabe (2009) also notes that "the key characteristics associated with automaticity, aside from speed, are that we cannot stop ourselves from carrying out the process and we cannot introspect on the process" (p. 27). If students develop automaticity, they can focus on meaning.

■ **Give students practice in quick reads for a specific purpose.**

DI students can benefit from practice in skimming and scanning texts, particularly to assess if the text would be a useful resource for a particular research topic that they will be writing on.

Goal 5: Build Students' Academic Vocabulary

It takes so long reading. I keep having to look up all the words.

—first-year developmental immigrant student

Challenge

Keith Folse (2004) argues that, for years, second language instructors deemphasized vocabulary learning while second language learners have been very concerned with learning more vocabulary. It was thought by instructors that context clues and constant language input led naturally to vocabulary acquisition. However, more current research has found that more direct instruction in vocabulary is crucial to language learning (Folse, 2004).

Suggested Approaches

DI students need direct focus and instruction on vocabulary as they build their academic language skills.

■ **Allow dictionary use.**

Advanced ESL dictionaries have limited defining vocabularies. Definitions are written using only words from a 2,000-word defining vocabulary. In this way, the students can understand definitions without looking up words found in the definition. Native language dictionaries should not be discouraged if context clues are not helping students to figure out word meaning.

■ **Ask students to generate and group vocabulary by where such vocabulary is used.**

Word rods are plastic rods that contain different words on each of their four sides. Reading Rods brand works well for many activities with DI students, and the rods are color-coded by part of speech. They can be used with DI students to build vocabulary and awareness of audience: The instructor can pull a noun, verb, or adjective out of a bag (it is best, at least in the beginning, to limit the activity to one part of speech at a time) and ask students to brainstorm synonyms. The class can then categorize the synonyms according to level of formality and type of context (Brown, 2009). Words from this activity could also be chosen from a class reading.

■ **Consider creating a word wall.**

If possible, instructors and/or students or groups of students can post key vocabulary words on a bulletin board or wall of the classroom with index cards or poster board. As an ongoing activity, this can help students see how much vocabulary they've acquired and encourage them to use these words appropriately in class discussions or in-class writing (perhaps earning participation points for correct use). Words can be grouped by subject area or part of speech, or they could be listed as word families.

■ **Utilize the Academic Word List (AWL).**

Avril Coxhead's Academic Word List (2000) is a list of words that occur with high frequency across academic subject areas. We have found that by focusing on these words, students can learn a high percentage of the words that they will encounter most frequently in academic contexts. The website www.academicvocabulary exercises.com offers online practice with these words. In addition, the vocabprofile feature of the Compleat Lexical Tutor (www.lextutor.ca) allows instructors or students to paste text and have its vocabulary analyzed. Words will be highlighted and noted as from one of the general service lists (which are more basic lists), the AWL, or off-list. This is extremely useful for determining the difficulty of a text or determining which words to teach. In addition, student writing can be entered into the profiler so that students can see the level of vocabulary they are using.

■ **Utilize an online concordance.**

Students can benefit from the use of an online concordance (Yoon & Hirvela, 2004; Kaur & Hegelheimer, 2005), which displays all uses of a particular word in a corpus (a large collection of texts) in a particular language. Students can then see how the word is typically used in the language. Yoon & Hirvela (2004) found that the use of a concordance by intermediate and advanced ESL students at a large U.S. university "was particularly beneficial for acquiring common usage of words, which resulted in their increased confidence about L2 writing" (2004, p. 277). A concordance can also be used to help differentiate usage between similar words. Excellent tutorials on the practical uses of concordances can be found at www.bu.edu/celop/mll/tutorials/pdf_public/concordance.pdf and in *A Practical Guide to Using Computers in Language Teaching* (de Szendeffy, 2005).

■ **Provide students with online options for creating flashcards, self quizzes, and quizzes to share with the class.**

Such options are an enjoyable and easy way to review. Students can quiz themselves or make puzzles to share with the class. They can also make online flashcards or a variety of word search and crossword puzzles, inserting the vocabulary and definitions they would like to use.

■ **Use reading and writing in combination to build vocabulary.**

Gabriella Nuttall (2005) recommends a series of reading and writing activities to develop students' vocabulary. Students first freewrite on a writing prompt (she uses a question about school violence) on a topic students will then read about. Students then discuss their freewrites in groups, as the instructor circulates and notes on the board words students used incorrectly. The class can then work with the instructor to clarify meaning and use of these words. Students then read two or three articles on the topic, highlighting what they believe to be key words. Working as a class, they try to determine meaning from context and then create a word list with sample sentences from the text. This process of vocabulary development may continue with a textbook excerpt or academic article on the topic, summary writing, group discussion, and essay question creation. Students could then write an essay based on one of the questions they created.

Goal 6: Improve Students' Screen Literacy

It's true. I found it on the Internet.

first-year developmental immigrant student

Challenge

DI students can be extremely comfortable with computers. Many use Facebook, YouTube, email, and the Internet multiple times a day. However, they usually lack a critical eye toward what they discover online. They seem to view the computer as a single source, rather than questioning the validity and authority of the individual websites they use.

Suggested Approaches

DI students need practice viewing Internet resources with a critical eye.

- **Provide practice in evaluating web sources.**

DI students need to understand the difference between Internet address endings (such as .com, .gov, .org, .net, .edu), and how these endings can hint at the validity of the information on a site. Cornell University Library provides a useful online guide for evaluating websites (www.library.cornell.edu/olinuris/ref/webcrit. html), as do many campus web pages.

- **Teach students how to use the campus' online library resources.**

DI students need to know how to use campus library search engines, such as ProQuest. Campus library staff can often provide lessons on the use of online resources during a class.

- **Teach critical evaluation by exposing students to "bogus" websites.**

Many websites are intentionally misleading (Troutner, 2009), and presenting them to students without initially telling them they are misleading can lead to productive (and entertaining) class discussion.

- **Consider a debate project that links a core course with a writing course.**

Linking assignments across courses can allow students to read and write more deeply on a topic. In the American Studies Cluster on our campus, students break into groups to debate current controversial American topics (such as gun control and whether or not college athletes should be paid). Students research their topics in the reading class, formally debate them in American Studies, and then write argumentative essays on the same topic in the writing class. In this way, students develop background knowledge, have the time to research and think extensively on the topic, and present an argument in writing after having argued it orally, which is a strength for DI students.

DI students can improve their academic reading and critical-thinking skills by working with authentic texts, learning and applying specific reading skills to these texts, and making reading-writing connections. For DI students, building academic literacy must continue throughout their four years of college. In this way, they become true members of the academic discourse community and form identities as college students who have valuable opinions and skills.

Additional Useful Websites

- **Elliot Aronson's Jigsaw classroom**
  www.jigsaw.org
  Useful guide to the jigsaw method of cooperative learning.

- **Who Reads Difficult Text? Your Students Can! by David Reynolds**
  www.cfkeep.org/html/snapshot.php?id=19602456148344
  Excellent resource for teaching reading strategies.

- **Instructional Strategies Online Saskatoon Public Schools**
  http://olc.spsd.sk.ca/DE/PD/Instr/
  Resources for many key instructional strategies useful for the teaching of reading.

- **Training Students for Literature Circles by Rita McLary**
  www.scholastic.com
  Search for this article on scholastic.com; useful tips for introducing literature circles.

- **The Basics of Effective Learning by Meg Keeley**
  www.bucks.edu/~specpop/annotate-ex.htm
  Useful tips on how to annotate text; sample annotated text included.

- **Online Speed Reading Lessons by Kris Madden**
  www.krismadden.com/on-speed-reading/

- **Timed Reading Exercises**
  www.readingsoft.com
  http://college.cengage.com/collegesurvival/watkins/learning_companion/1e/students/timed_reading.html

- **The Longman Advanced Dictionary of American English**
  www.ldoceonline.com
  This online dictionary contains a 2,000 word defining vocabulary, so it's easy for students to use and comprehend.

- **A Concordance Site from the United Arab Emirates University**
  www.ugru.uaeu.ac.ae/concordance/
  Useful way for students to see how a word is really used.

- **Sites for Making Flashcards and Quizzes**
  www.flashcardmachine.com
  http://puzzlemaker.discoveryeducation.com/

- **Intentionally Misleading Websites**
  Dog Island www.thedogisland.com, Jackalope Conspiracy www.sudftw.com/jackcon.htm, and Tree Octopus zapatopi.net/treeoctopus
  Useful for a discussion of how to evaluate websites.

Chapter 8

Teaching Writing

KEY POINTS

☞ Writing is the subject that many developmental immigrant students fear the most.

☞ A writing course for DI students needs to emphasize critical thinking, detailed development, and logical organization.

☞ Students need to understand that writing is an academic literacy skill that they will need in college and in their professional careers.

When I was in high school I thought I was the best writer because my ESL teacher used to tell me all my four years in high school told me I was the best. Then after year ago I attend to [college] and find out that I was the worst writer ever and I have long way to learn how to write an essay.

Because of my English skill was not even approach standard, I did not have to write many essays in high school. Usually two essays per year for me were plenty because I would spend at least a week to write a one page essay. Even my senior project's paper was only two pages long . . .

—*first-year developmental immigrant students*

The writing expectations of college instructors are often vastly different from those of the high school teachers these students have encountered (Allison, 2009). Tony Silva (1993) notes that second language writers have all the writing challenges of native-speaking developmental students (such as difficulty composing, planning, generating, organizing, and expressing ideas effectively), yet to a much higher degree. The jump to college writing for DI students is especially hard, but it can also be an opportunity for tremendous academic growth when students are guided and supported in making the academic leap.

Writing is the subject developmental immigrant students often fear most. They know that they have trouble with writing, but they can't define these struggles. There are many reasons for this: some students become so focused on grammar, word choice, and sentence-level writing (Shaughnessy, 1977; Urzua, 1987; Durst, 1999) that they neglect to consider overall essay structure and find it harder to fully develop their ideas in writing. This may be due to the more complex intellectual demands of writing in a language they are still learning. Many DI students also come from middle school and high school classes that emphasized grammar and "correctness" at the sentence level but did not focus on or provide feedback on content or organization, as the teacher may have been too busy "fitting everything else in." Alternately, some students may have received little to no feedback on grammar, content, or structure in previous English classes and were rewarded simply for getting the assignment done and being well-behaved (Harklau, 2000), rather than for the quality of the finished product. Other students may have simply been required to provide short answers (rather than paragraphs or essays), or they wrote essays by answering a series of questions and arranging these answers in five-paragraph format (Allison, 2009).

The overarching goals of writing instruction for DI students entering college, then, should be to make them more comfortable and confident in their writing, to teach them to work with their strengths and to identify and develop strategies to improve targeted skills. It is imperative that DI students learn to respond to and work with texts in their writing, as most have written almost exclusively about personal experiences in high school (Muchinsky & Tangren, 1999) because this is often the high school curriculum. College writing requires analysis and incorporation of outside texts (Blanton, 1999).

DI students require multiple semesters of writing instruction. In the first semester of basic writing (also called developmental or remedial writing), they should move from paragraph to essay and from personal writing to analytical writing to writing that incorporates research. In first-year composition, they should write longer, more complex essays that respond to the ideas in a text or in multiple texts. An additional second-semester reading-writing course would further help DI students develop their critical-thinking and writing skills.

Essential to all classes is the writing tutorial. An effective tutorial is a conversation that can function as a scaffold for students (Weissberg & Hochhalter, 2006; Williams, 2004), allowing students to clarify and deepen their thinking. Students should meet with the same tutor each week to develop a rapport that would allow for deeper levels of discussion and revision and more personalized instruction. Also essential is that writing class time be focused on writing, with students actively working on their writing in class (a computer lab is invaluable) and discussing and reading each other's work as well.

Most of all, students need to understand that writing is a critical skill for college and beyond. Many students believe that since they aren't English majors, they won't need strong writing skills in college. An examination of college syllabi in all subject areas will reveal that writing is an important component of almost every college course.

This chapter focuses primarily on activities and approaches suitable for a first-semester basic writing class. Because this class introduces students to college writing expectations, its activities and emphasis should focus on essay structure, detailed development, clarity, and increasing comfort in expression to give students the confidence they need to share their voices with the world. Additional activities in this chapter are suitable for a first-year composition course, a reading-writing course, a content course, or a writing tutorial.

Goal 1: Make Students More Comfortable with Writing

What I hate about writing is that the way you speak is not the way you write. So it's sometimes hard to get your grammer right because you are use to speaking different.

What I hate about writing: grammer and rules. Expressing my thoughts is a very difficult thing for me. Having to write them down on paper is even harder.

—DI student responses to first day of class writing questionnaire

---

Challenge

Most students dread writing. DI students often view writing as a series of grammar rules they can't master and an accumulation of vocabulary words they don't have, so many enter a writing course saying that they hate to write. Like most Generation 1.5 and developmental students, they quickly become frustrated at their inability to express complex ideas in English and are highly critical of themselves and their errors in writing (Durst, 1999; Shaughnessy, 1977; Urzua, 1987). Many DI students are also afraid to reveal a "voice," perhaps because asserting one's own voice in writing is not culturally practiced or because of a lack of self-confidence in U.S. academics or because they are still in the complex process of forming their own identities.

Suggested Approaches

Teachers and researchers in developmental education frequently note that because many developmental students have often had negative experiences in writing, it is particularly important to create a positive and supportive environment in any course that involves writing. Krashen has stressed the importance of lowering the affective filter in order for students to learn a second language more effectively (1981b). The affective filter can be defined as the "level of stress, anxiety, fear or frustration the student feels when given a learning task" (Sadek, 2008). Although the validity of Krashen's linguistic theories may be debated, it seems clear that in order to help developmental students gain confidence in their abilities and improve their skills, teachers must first create an environment in which students can view themselves and the writing process (and the relationship between themselves and writing) in a positive light. Students need to become comfortable in the classroom and with their classmates in order to become risk-takers: trying out ideas, finding their voices, and learning to express their thoughts clearly and powerfully.

In any class that involves writing, the atmosphere needs to be purposely created, beginning with the first meeting. Students need to feel comfortable with each other in order to become more comfortable talking about and sharing their writing. Students need to be comfortable with the instructor and sense his/her expertise, support, and respect. William Kelly, co-author of the developmental writing text *Odyssey* (2006), notes that a developmental writing teacher needs to be "encouraging, respectful [and] lighthearted" (Roberts, 2003). In addition, the instructor must also be well-prepared and confident in his or her abilities, someone the students can view as knowledgeable in writing and supportive of learning. Institutions need to seek out writing teachers who project this confidence and encouragement in the classroom.

■ **Provide early opportunities for students to become more comfortable with each other.**

It is particularly important in a writing class, where students will share their writings, that students are comfortable with each other. We have found that the best writing classroom icebreaker activities involving writing are those that immediately get students writing and talking about the ideas they've written and their relationship with writing. Students could complete a first day of class survey (such as the sample included in Appendix 8a), share their responses with a partner, introduce that partner to the class, and then engage in a discussion about their attitudes and beliefs about writing.

■ **Provide early opportunities for students to become more comfortable talking about writing.**

It is also important to get students thinking about *how* they best learn, work and write (Chamot & O'Malley, 1994; Porter & van Dommelen, 2004). By sharing their attitudes, strategies, and experiences, the class can begin to feel that they're "all in the same boat" and, more important, that they can learn strategies and skills to be able to write successfully and confidently. Metacognitive skills are essential for any successful student, and classroom activities can be helpful to create this confidence and awareness.

- Ask student groups to generate advice for common writing problems. One useful way to get students to view writing as a skill they can master and a quick way for instructors to informally assess students' metacognitive skills is through an "advice" activity. Provide groups of students (3–4 per group works well) with a chart of common student problems, as shown in Figure 8.1, and ask them to work as a group to suggest strategies they've tried or heard of to help overcome each problem.

This activity allows the instructor (who can circulate among groups as they work) to quickly see which students are aware of or are using various writing strategies and which students simply list a vague "ask a teacher" as their solution for each problem. It also offers the opportunity to discuss the difference between revising (making changes in content and organization) and editing (correcting grammar and surface errors). Group lists can be collated on the board for discussion. Students can also be given a list (see Figure 8.2 on pages 109–11) for future reference, perhaps with the addition of student-generated responses.

■ **Create immediate opportunities to learn about the students as writers.**

It is essential for instructors to see students' individual writing strengths and weaknesses as soon as possible in order for effective and personalized instruction to take place. In addition, instructors emphasize the importance of writing when students communicate in writing from the first day.

- Collect writing samples from students on the first day. Prompts for writing samples on the first day can be as simple as "Write a paragraph introducing yourself to the class." A more complex prompt could ask students how they feel about writing, what their past experience has been with writing, and what they hope to learn in class. Students could also write about their names and the meanings, associations, or history behind them (Spack, 2008). These samples can give instructors insight into students' writing fluency and attitudes toward writing, especially if they observe students as

FIGURE 8.1
Chart of Common Student Problems

Name _____

Advice for Writers

DIRECTIONS: Work with your group to brainstorm and list advice for each of these common writing problems.

I can't get started. I see a blank page and can't write anything!	*I can't organize my writing.*
I'm not good at revising.	*I make too many mistakes.*

FIGURE 8.2
Common Writing Problems and How to Solve Them

Name _____

I can't get started! I see a blank page and can't write <u>anything</u>!

- **TALK about your ideas with someone.** Take notes as you talk. Your partner can ask you questions as you discuss your ideas.
- **Try different forms of PREWRITING.**
  Brainstorm: Make a list of everything you can think of. Choose some ideas as possible topics, then talk about a few of your ideas. Choose one topic and brainstorm on it further. Group these ideas.
  Freewrite: Write whatever is in your head (including "I can't think of anything to write"). Don't stop writing. After five or ten minutes, read what you wrote and circle your favorite ideas.
  Cluster: This can really help you narrow down a large topic. Create a web, grouping related ideas together. One branch of your cluster can become the start of your paragraph or essay.
- **Get comfortable!** Use a small notepad if it's less intimidating, or write your notes on the computer (you can even send yourself or a friend an email!) if that's less stressful for you.
- **Write when you get the idea.** Don't wait until the last minute! When you're given an assignment, immediately start to think about possible topics. You can then write down ideas as you get them. Jot something down on a napkin in the cafeteria or on a scrap of paper in the workout room—whatever works, wherever you are! (Just be sure to put your notes somewhere safe so you can use them later!)
- **Keep a journal!** The more writing you do, the more possible topics you will have when it's time to write for class.

I can't organize my writing!

- **Make sure you've done enough brainstorming.** If you don't have enough ideas when you start, you'll write ideas in your paper in whatever order they come in your head—not a good way to stay focused!
- **Group your ideas!** This important step will help you see relationships and get organized!

- **Try different types of graphic organizers** Try a few of the organizers (webs, traditional outlines, etc.) you were given in class, or make one of your own that helps you to visualize your topic sentence and major and minor details.
- **Physically move your ideas around.** Put each idea on a different index card, and arrange the cards until you've created a logical pattern.
- **Use color.** Color-coding your major and minor points can help you see organization.
- **Make sure you follow your plan!** Many students fill out their graphic organizers beautifully, then write a paper that doesn't follow the plan at all! It's natural to make some changes as you write your paper, but if you stray too far from your organizer, your finished paper may not clearly back up your point. You may have to go back and work more on your organizer, then write again/revise your writing.
- **Keep checking!** Make sure each point backs up your topic sentence or thesis, and be certain that you have enough relevant details for each point.
- **After you finish writing, draw the organization of the paragraph/essay you've just created.** Does it look similar to the organizer with which you began? Does it make sense? Is it logical and easy to follow?

I'm not good at revising.

- **Put your paragraph or essay away for a day or two.** When you look at it again, you'll be able to be more objective.
- **Read your writing out loud, slowly.** Note where ideas are missing or unclear. Listen to see if your ideas flow well and all relate to your topic sentence/thesis.
- **Read your writing to someone else, or ask someone else to read it.** Ask your reader tell you what is unclear. It's best if you are the only one to write on your paper. Listen to what others say, and then write the changes you think are best.
- **Don't work sentence-by-sentence in the revising stage.** Look at the big picture. Expect to go over your paper several times, making global improvements each time. Change the big things (strengthening the structure of your argument, adding transitions and coherence) at this stage.

I make too many grammatical and spelling mistakes.

- **Do your best while you write your draft, but don't focus so much on grammar and spelling that you can't get your ideas down.** It's most important to write an organized paragraph or essay first. You can then polish the paper's grammar and spelling (which are important to the final product).

- **Keep a record of the types of grammatical errors that give you trouble, and then choose one error at a time to look for in your writing.** Write the name of your most common error (run-on, verb tense, etc.) on the top of your paper. Then hunt for (and correct) that error throughout your paper. Write your next most common error at the top of the page, and repeat the process. Attack two or three of your most common errors in this way.

- **Read your paper backward, sentence-by-sentence (and preferably out loud).** Examining each sentence out of context can help you spot mistakes.

- Use spell check, a dictionary, or a list of commonly misspelled words and commonly confused homonyms to check your work. **Each time you edit a paper, choose three words whose spelling you want to learn.** Memorize the spelling for these words.

- Notice the types of spelling errors you make. **Take the time to learn rules** ("i" before "e" except after "c"...) that cause you trouble.

---

they write. (Do students stop and start? Write a sentence or two quickly, and then sit and wait for "writing time" to be over? Take a long time to get started? Hunch their shoulders? Start immediately and write furiously until you say "stop"?) Writing samples can be analyzed for organization, focus, detail, and grammar difficulties, and instructors could choose to respond to each in writing.

- <u>Survey students.</u> It's particularly important for instructors of courses that involve writing to find out as much as they can about the students in the first few days/weeks of class. The results of surveys given in a basic writing class (such as samples in Appendix 8a) can be shared with other instructors in a course cluster. Instructors can write content-based responses on students' forms and make copies to keep for themselves. They can also write questions on the forms asking for more information, or they can ask students to tell more orally, creating an immediate dialogue early in the semester.

■ **Create manageable assignments, and teach students how to manage their work and time.**

Many DI students get overwhelmed when told to write a paragraph or essay. Presenting writing assignments as a series of small steps and creating due dates for each step can make an assignment much more manageable for students and can lead to student success.

- Break writing assignments into steps, with separate due dates for each step. Dividing the assignment into steps can allow instructors to informally assess and provide immediate feedback at any or all stages, ensuring a better end product and more confident student writers. Frequent feedback (from teachers, from peers) at all stages of the writing process and on content, organization, and detail is what will allow student writers to develop their skills. Instructors in the content areas can consult with writing tutors or basic writing instructors to determine manageable steps.

- Incorporate writing checklists and set clear expectations for each writing assignment on the assignment sheet. Utilizing writing checklists (with criteria such as "My essay contains a clear, specific thesis statement that contains the topic + what I will show or prove about the topic," "I use specific examples that support my thesis statement," and "My essay uses transition words to move smoothly between ideas") during the revision process and including these, along with clear written expectations on assignment handouts, can empower students and help them succeed. Grading rubrics can reflect the content of the checklists.

- Gradually transition students into writing in response to text. In college, DI students in particular need extensive practice in writing with and responding to texts, as their previous writing experiences in English have almost exclusively been personal narratives. We have found that DI students can benefit from a few writing experiences in which they write about topics they already know in a more analytic way that is in a non-narrative style before they move on to responding to and/or incorporating the writing of others. In their second-semester composition course and their reading-writing course (International Literature and Film) at Penn State Brandywine, students write almost exclusively in response to text. If possible, students should have a choice of topic and should have preferably brainstormed on more than one topic before choosing one to write about.

Goal 2: Develop Competence in Rhetorical Structure and Detailed Development

Sometimes I see a student's writing and wonder, "Where do I start?" The ideas are all over the place, and he or she doesn't even have a clear topic sentence. Everything's jumbled together or not explained.

—new peer writing tutor

Challenge

Many languages and cultures consider the straightforward academic writing style common in the United States, where one states a main point, backs it up with specific, detailed examples, and then essentially restates the main point with more of a "so what" ending, to be immature and the sign of a poor writer. A strong writer, in many cultures, is one who talks around a point, who is more obtuse, and who therefore doesn't insult the intelligence of the reader, who is expected to be smart enough to determine the meaning. Rhetorical structures in different cultures and languages can be very different, as revealed by Kaplan (1966). Furthermore, many cultures do not have the same sense of intellectual property. It is acceptable and expected in these cultures to write the words of others without citation and to expect the reader to understand that these are not the writer's words. (This last issue is discussed in Chapter 5.)

Suggested Approaches

Sample essays, graphic organizers, and direct instruction in the elements of an academic essay can help the developmental immigrant student master such rhetorical structures as comparison/contrast, cause/effect, and argument. Analysis and graphic representation of professional writing samples and the students' own writing can help in their writing organization and reading comprehension. In a basic writing class, focusing first on writing a paragraph and then moving to a five- or six-paragraph essay format can help students grasp organizational concepts. Students who are used to writing essays in high school may balk at starting with paragraphs, but they soon find that the smaller assignments allow them to focus more on structure and detail. In a first-year composition course and in content courses, students can move beyond this basic structure to more sophisticated patterns that fit best with more complex assignments. Teaching the five-paragraph essay (and moving from writing the single paragraph to writing five- or six-paragraph essays in a basic writing class) is becoming an increasingly prevalent method in developmental writing texts, but it is not without controversy (see Novick, 2001; Wesley, 2000; and Nunnally, 1991), as it is often considered too "rigid" or "artificial." However, most developmental instructors agree that it is a useful reference point for students, particularly for developmental immigrant students, as long as it is used as a model and springboard for longer and more complex writing assignments in higher-level classes. The five-paragraph essay is not acceptable in discipline-specific writing courses.

■ **Provide several strong samples of each rhetorical structure.**

Many writing textbooks and websites provide sample paragraphs and essays for different rhetorical structures. Sharing and discussing these with students can demonstrate more variety within the basic structure, making it more likely students will find a sample they can relate to, and reinforcing structural concepts learned in class.

■ **Model active reading and text analysis.**

Because developmental immigrant students are "ear learners" rather than "eye learners" of English (Reid, 1997) and because they often have weak reading skills, it is beneficial to sometimes read sample paragraphs and essays to students as well as to have students read silently on their own. Instructors can model active reading by emphasizing transition words, counting out main points on their fingers, asking questions after a main point followed by details, and working with the class to outline the structure and main points of the sample paragraph or essay on the board. Students can also mark up the sample essay or text to highlight its structure and message. The same can then be done with their own writing or the writing of a peer (in a whole class, small group or pairs, or by the instructor or the student using an overhead projector). This text analysis can be reinforced in reading and content-area classes, and texts from the content course can be analyzed in the writing course as well.

■ **Instruct students in the use of a variety of graphic organizers.**

Planning an essay graphically after brainstorming can help students organize and develop their writing before drafting, resulting in a much stronger rough draft. However, because students have different learning styles and writing processes, it is important to help students find the best way to graphically organize their ideas. One useful activity is to discuss the different ways instructors write notes on the board—a science instructor may label his or her points (a, b, c, 1, 2, 3) in outline form, while an English instructor may simply write and circle key words in seemingly random places on the board or draw arrows between ideas. (Of course, this is stereotypical—but students will often share the board-writing style of individual instructors during this discussion.) Students can then look at a list of graphic organizers (samples can be found in Appendix 8b) and use their brainstorming as a starting point to complete the organizer they find most useful. The class can discuss their organizer choices and their growing awareness of their own thinking processes and writing styles. The graphic organizer is an important step in the writing process: it allows students to make major changes in content and organization early on, rather than after having written a lengthy text.

■ **Use video clips to reinforce or introduce rhetorical styles.**

Many rhetorical styles can be illustrated with videos found online. Several sites used by Linn Lisher (2009) at Bucks County Community College are listed at the end of this chapter.

■ **Provide explicit instruction in the elements of an academic essay.**

Many DI students need direct instruction in the parts of an academic essay in order to be successful. (see Appendix 8d for samples of final writing assignments).

- *Develop students' ability to craft strong topic sentences and strong thesis statements.* A topic sentence or thesis statement can be defined to students as the TOPIC + what will be SHOWN or PROVEN with this topic. Students should practice narrowing and focusing topics into supportable topic sentences and thesis statements and identifying strong topic sentences and sentences that are too narrow or factual to be a good topic sentence.
- *Develop students' understanding of the importance of an engaging introduction.* One way to stress the importance of a strong introduction is to describe it as the hook used to lure in a reader. DI students often feel that they can't start writing their essays until they have come up with an introduction. This is not the case. It can be beneficial for students with a strong thesis statement to write their body paragraphs first and then add the introduction once the essay is more fully formed.
- *Increase students' awareness of and ability to use transition words and structure-essential vocabulary consistently and effectively.* Requiring students to identify transition words in their writing and the writing of others and discussing their purpose and effectiveness can help students become more consistent and comfortable with their own use of transition words. In addition, content-essential transition words should be introduced with each rhetorical structure. For example, cause/effect words for cause/effect essays should be explicitly taught, and students need to be able to effectively use "hedging" words (Hinkel, 2005) and persuasive language in argumentative writing.

- *Develop students' ability to produce forceful conclusions.* An essay's conclusion needs to be a strong final thought. Developmental writers often "parrot" the thesis statement in their conclusions, simply copying (or nearly copying) their thesis statement as the final sentence of the essay. Students need to think of a conclusion as a "so what?" ending, something that provides a final thought or a statement of what was learned. By concluding with a thought that answers a "so what"-type question (*Why was what I told you important? / How does it apply to the reader? / What lessons were learned? / What judgment can I make? / What prediction/hope does this lead to?*), students can conclude with higher-level thinking, rather than a simple summary statement. Directly teaching students how to identify and write strong conclusions can help them throughout their academic careers and beyond.

- *Help students understand the reader-writer conversation.* Students need to understand that the difference between writing and speaking is that in a conversation, the listener can ask questions to get more information or clarification. In writing, the writer needs to *anticipate* these questions and have them already answered for the reader. By sharing their writing with a partner, students can ask each other questions to elicit more detail or clarification that can then be added to the writing.

Goal 3: Use Oral Language Skills as a Strength

You can buy used college test books instead of new ones because the used books are less expansive than the new wants.

—*first-year developmental immigrant student writing sample*

Challenge

DI students make many errors in their writing because they write what they hear. The student quotation above contains many errors that would not be caught by computer spell check. In addition, DI students often write in short, choppy, "talky" sentences that contain many generalizations and little development. One reason for this is that they are still learning the grammar and vocabulary of English; they write simple sentences because they're uncomfortable with more complex grammatical structures, and they write more generally because they don't know more specific vocabulary.

This lack of vocabulary knowledge is intrinsically linked to weak reading skills. DI students also tend to write in a "talky," general manner because they are more comfortable with oral, two-way conversations than the more one-sided, more polished presentation of written English.

Suggested Approaches

DI students can be taught to use their oral skills as a strength to enrich and flesh out their writing. In addition, simply creating awareness in students of WHY they make the written errors they do—how many of these errors are created by writing what they hear—often allows them to become better editors of their own writing because they then know what to look for.

■ **Designate student "note takers" to help students see their own natural organization or express their ideas more clearly.**

If student writers are having a lot of difficulty organizing their ideas, it's sometimes helpful for them to cover up their ideas and orally answer the question, "What is your paper about?" or "What do you want to say in your paper?" Students (or the instructor) can then make an outline of the students' main ideas as they expressed them, creating the start of a graphic organizer that can be fleshed out and followed during the drafting stage. In addition, if sections of a DI student's writing are "non-English" and difficult or impossible to comprehend, simply covering up the writing and saying, "Tell me in your own words what you're saying here" can help the student use clearer language to express ideas, and then writing what was said.

■ **Discuss peer response as a class to a (willing!) student's writing.**

On days that students are expected to bring rough drafts to class, ask for a volunteer whose writing can be the topic of a class-wide peer response. Photocopy the paper, give each student a copy, read it out loud, and then have students read it to themselves again silently. Completing a peer response sheet and giving oral feedback as a class can model real-life, useful peer response and help all students better respond to each other.

■ **Encourage students to read their writing out loud to self-correct grammatical errors.**

Some grammatical errors that DI students make can be self-corrected when students read their own writing out loud.

■ **Encourage students to develop vocabulary during writing revision.**

When students revise their writing, they are usually searching for just the right word to get their ideas across. This is one of the best ways for students to acquire new vocabulary, when they have a specific need for a specific word and it is relevant to them. Encourage students who are stumped by word choice while writing to fill in a word close to what they want and circle it, write two or more words they might use and circle them, or even write the needed word in their native language (Brown, 2009). In this way, students do not lose writing fluency and can then discuss word choice in revision with other students, with the instructor, or with a writing tutor.

Goal 4: Develop Students' Cognitive and Metacognitive Skills

In high school I always thought writing an essay the important part is not the introduction, so I just casual to write a paragraph that has no thesis, no structure, and no clear thrust. But the grade I got make me feel stirring, the teacher always just hand back with no correction and no comments. That make me feel if the teachers did not say anything about my essay which means it is find [fine].

—*first-year developmental immigrant student*

Challenge

DI students may enter college without having had the experience of receiving feedback on the *content* of their writing and without a clear sense of what writing strategies work for them. Students usually expect college to be "the thirteenth grade" and don't understand that their writing will be assessed on the basis of their expressed *ideas* and that they will be expected to take more control of their own learning.

Suggested Approaches

An important shift DI students must make is that writing is itself a *thinking process*. Students must begin to view writing as a forum for the discovery and discussion of ideas and of academic discourse. Instructors should work (within the course of a semester) to move students from writing from experience, to writing in response to reading, to writing with research. Metacognitive skills are also critical for DI students in college, so that they begin to understand how they think and learn best.

■ **Respond to the content of student writing.**

Instructors should provide feedback orally (in informal in-class conferences) and in writing (in the margins, in an end note) to the content of student writing. The content of sample essays and class readings should also be discussed. In her book *Response to Student Writing: Implications for Second Language Students*, Ferris (2003) models for teachers both margin comments (which mimic a reader-writer conversation) and end-note comments. It can be impractical for instructors to comment this extensively on every rough draft, but these types of comments are necessary periodically. It is essential, however, that if students are given feedback orally, that the instructor be sure that the students are making clear notations in their drafts of each bit of feedback. If this is difficult for a particular student to do, the instructor may choose to make margin notes as he or she talks with the student. This type of feedback can also be made in conversation by writing tutors trained in working with DI students.

■ **Use clear rubrics to provide feedback on student writing.**

Rubrics that reflect content, organization, development, and grammar can help students understand the strengths and weaknesses of their paragraphs and essays in a useful way. Many rubrics can be found online. Rubrics that may be useful in a basic writing class are included in Figure 8.3 on pages 120–21.

■ **Engage students in real written dialogue.**

Writing about topics that are important to them and sharing their writing with real audiences creates a sense of purpose for students. The school newspaper, campus literary magazine, or an in-house publication can be powerful student platforms. In addition, the website ThisIBelieve.org contains thousands of essays by people from all walks of life about their deepest beliefs and life lessons. It is searchable by theme and includes recordings of many of the authors reading their own work. Students can submit their own essays to the site.

■ **Read strong (student-generated) final drafts out loud and discuss as a class.**

It can be highly motivating and useful for students to read strong writing by the class after each assignment. Papers can be photocopied with student names omitted and read out loud (with student permission), so the class can discuss the writing's strengths. Varying the student authors with each assignment can encourage students in their work. (If the topic of the writing is personal or sensitive, it should not be shared with the class.) Emailing or pulling aside students for permission to anonymously (if desired) share their writing can be encouraging to the student and give a real-world feel to the assignments. In addition, a class book can be a culminating project, where each student chooses his or her favorite piece of writing for inclusion and copies of the book are distributed to all students.

FIGURE 8.3
Sample Rubric

Paragraph Evaluation

Scale

10	Excellent
9	Very Good
8	Satisfactory
7	Weak, but acceptable
6	Needs serious improvement
0–5	Unsatisfactory

Criteria

Topic sentence   _____
Focus on topic   _____
Detailed development   _____
Organization and transition   _____
Use of standard English   _____

               Total = _____ x 2 = _____ (Grade)

Comments:

Essay Evaluation

Scale

10	Excellent
9	Very Good
8	Satisfactory
7	Weak, but acceptable
6	Needs serious improvement
0–5	Unsatisfactory

Criteria

Introduction	_____	x 1 = _____
Thesis statement	_____	x 2 = _____
Well-developed body paragraphs	_____	x 3 = _____
Clear transitions	_____	x 1 = _____
Concluding paragraph	_____	x 1 = _____
Standard English	_____	x 2 = _____

Total   = _____

Comments:

■ **Provide multiple opportunities for students to reflect on their writing and writing processes.**

Students can reflect on their writing during many stages by writing down their thoughts. During the planning, drafting, and revising stages, students can complete written reflections (a sample is included in Appendix 8c) and then discuss (in small groups or as a whole class) what strategies are working/not working for them. At the end of the semester, a final reflection form (see Appendix 8d for a form useful in basic writing and Appendix 8c for one useful in first-year composition) can help students see how much they've grown.

■ **Provide opportunities for students to talk about their writing strategies and give advice to other writers.**

During peer response, students can suggest strategies for their peers to try and can share ideas that worked for them. Students can also share and discuss what they've written in the reflections described above. Peer response work can be done in pairs (students can be required to switch partners until they've worked with two or three different people) or in small groups (students can be required to bring a photocopy of their handwritten or typed drafts for each member of the group). Instructors could ask that students fill out the response forms and hand them in or give them to the authors (who can then attach them to final drafts). Alternately, peer response could be more informal if students appear to be on task and productive. Students could also work on their drafts on the computers (if class is in a computer lab), with peers providing informal or formal feedback.

■ **Conference with students about their writing.**

DI students can find class periods that focus on giving feedback to rough drafts extremely useful. As students work in peer response groups, the instructor can circulate and provide individual feedback to students. If volunteers or tutors are available to the instructor, they can be invited to circulate as well.

DI students can grow and thrive in a basic writing class that understands and addresses their needs and builds upon their strengths. As writing is a key college skill for college assessment, a strong foundation in writing can lead to a strong academic career.

Additional Useful Websites

- **Websites useful for demonstrating rhetorical structure**
  www.youtube.com *The Fresh Prince of Bel Air* intro: for illustrating narration
  www.howcast.com for illustrating process writing
  www.pbs.com for videos that can be used to create comparison/contrast charts

- **Where the hell is Matt?**
  www.wherethehellismatt.com
  Excellent discussion and writing prompt. Matt Harding has traveled around the world, filming himself dancing with local people. His entertaining videos are available on this site, and his essay (and his reading of this essay) can be found on www.ThisIBelieve.org.

Chapter 9

Teaching Grammar for Writing

KEY POINTS

☞ Most developmental immigrant students believe that any problems they have with writing are because of weak grammar skills.

☞ Students generally don't know why their grammar is weak; they usually cannot pinpoint any one problem.

☞ They are very appreciative when they do receive help with grammar.

☞ Grammar should be taught in relation to writing.

I want my English to get better. Because I'm in college and my English still not that good.

—first-year developmental immigrant student

By the time Generation 1.5 students get to college, they know that they have trouble with grammar, and they want to improve (Ferris, 2003). Shaughnessy observes that developmental students often find that their trouble with grammatical accuracy gets in the way of writing fluency and idea development, as they often start and restart individual sentences, trying to avoid grammatical errors (1977), and clearly these problems are true for DI students as well. In many cases though, DI students are not able to articulate their grammatical difficulties any more specifically than "grammar" or large categories such as "punctuation," which makes it difficult for them not to feel overwhelmed and frustrated at the scope of their perceived needs.

Instructors of DI students, too, can feel overwhelmed. Faced with papers riddled with grammatical errors and "non-English" sentences, many teachers don't know where to begin in instruction, what grammatical issues to emphasize, or what approaches to take. Instructors quickly find that students who can master a worksheet page (on past perfect tense, for example) or who can explain the rules for subject-verb agreement still do not produce writing that follows these rules. It seems clear that explicit knowledge (understanding the rules) does not equal implicit knowledge (spontaneous language production that follows these rules). Such experience may cause instructors to question how, when, or even IF to teach grammar in a writing class or in a separate or linked grammar class.

DI students are like Generation 1.5 and ESL students in that they *want* grammar instruction and *want* and *value* feedback on their written grammatical errors (Leki, 1990; Ferris, 1995; Ferris & Hedgcock, 2005), and a grammar-for-writing approach appears to work best to meet these students' needs in college (Ferris, 2002, 2003; Ferris & Hedgcock, 2005). Ferris (2002, 2003) and Ferris and Hedgcock (2005) assert that teacher feedback can make a difference in student progress. Many researchers and instructors make the case for focused grammar mini-lessons within a writing class (Ferris & Hedgcock, 2005), and many programs (Murie & Fitzpatrick, 2009; Goen-Salter, Porter, & vanDommelen, 2009), including our own American Studies Cluster, have found that a separate grammar course linked to a writing course and supported by writing tutors (in a learning or writing center, for example) can make a significant difference in student progress.

Ferris (2002) calls for " . . . the treatment of students' written error in a comprehensive and integrated way that assumes that such treatment involves not only teacher feedback and grammar instruction but also consciousness-raising, strategy training, and student accountability." This approach is the crux of teaching students self-editing skills and assumes that students can learn to actively notice and correct many of their own grammatical errors as a part of their learning process. Ellis's (2006) *weak interface position,* for example, posits that if learners have implicit knowledge, readiness to acquire, (and, many suggest, sufficient time), they will focus on language forms (as opposed to meaning) and be able to notice and usually correct their own written errors.

In order to make these self-corrections, DI students need to learn very specific editing strategies and practice them frequently in their own writing. However, they also need to understand that learning to self-edit is a long process. Grammar instruction and editing practice can occur in many classroom contexts (we advocate a 3-credit grammar course for the first semester), but they should also be a part of writing tutorials, usually for the duration of the students' college experience. With support in both the classroom and in tutorials, DI students can begin to internalize many grammatical rules that they have found problematic and can become better editors of their own writing.

Goal 1: Choose an Approach That Best Fits Your Student and Campus Needs

I want to learn pretty much everything . . .

—first-year DI student's written response to "What do you most want to learn in your grammar class this fall? Why?"

Challenge

Instructors and DI students know that the students have many grammatical needs; however, many campuses or programs do not have the funding or resources to offer a stand-alone grammar course for immigrant students, despite the evidence that more instruction over a longer period of time (as opposed to shorter, more intensive instruction, such as in a summer course) works best for language gains (Ellis, 2006).

Suggested Approaches

Sometimes it is necessary for faculty to start with a smaller course offering and build it up over time. As part of a large university, we have a large number of existing course numbers and have found that using an existing course number made it much easier to create our grammar course (which is 3 credits, and counts as an elective toward graduation). By working with what is available, instructors and administrators can start small (perhaps with a writing workshop or designated tutors) and keep records of program success (through pre- and post-tests, anecdotal evidence, faculty surveys, GPA improvement, retention rates, etc.) to make the case for additional programming. Some ways that grammar instruction can be incorporated into a DI student college program include:

■ **Mini-lessons within a basic writing or first-year composition class.**

These can be sequenced according to the grammar points and specific language needed for various writing tasks or on an "as needed" basis, depending on an instructor's findings of common errors in student writing. If many students in the class have the same language background, instructors may find (as we have found) that a resource such as *Learner English: A Teacher's Guide to Interference and Other Problems* (Swan & Smith, 2001) can provide some useful insight into common errors and difficulties students from that language background may have. (This text is also a useful tutor resource.) However, instructors must be careful that the writing class does not become a grammar class.

■ **A separate (or linked) grammar course.**

If the resources are available, this can be sequenced from global to more local errors, such as the approach found in many developmental writing texts, and, if possible, it should be linked to an existing basic writing class, first-year composition class, and/or a writing tutorial. (This is the approach our campus has found to be most effective.)

■ **A grammar or editing workshop.**

This can be an added-on for-credit "lab" component of a writing class, a weekly small-group one-credit (or two-credit class, as described in Murie & Fitzpatrick, 2009), or a grammar tutorial. If the meeting is purely elective and non-credit bearing, it is unlikely that students will follow through and commit time and effort to the workshop. However, this workshop could supplement mini-lessons within a writing class, particularly with students who are weakest in grammar.

■ **Individualized grammar instruction within a weekly (or twice weekly) writing tutorial.**

Writing tutors who meet with the same student each week can focus on a student's individual strengths and needs and can communicate with the writing teacher as needed. However, writing tutors must be certain that they do not spend so much time on grammar that content, organization, and development are not adequately addressed. In many cases, it may be useful to extend the amount of tutoring each week (perhaps from weekly to twice weekly) or to designate a separate grammar tutorial.

Goal 2: Develop Students' Awareness of Their Most Common and Most Serious Grammatical Errors

---

I want learn most about my writing, because I have been making a lots of mistakes.

—first-year DI student's written response to "What do you most want to learn in your grammar class this fall? Why?"

Challenge

Developmental immigrant students are very concerned about their grammar in writing, citing their numerous grammatical mistakes as evidence that they are "not good writers." Many times they cannot articulate exactly what areas of grammar they find particularly troublesome and cannot prioritize what errors to focus on first.

Suggested Approaches

When DI students are introduced to a basic concept of *noticing*, they can be visibly relieved. Although this does not solve students' grammatical problems, it can be an important first step. When an instructor acknowledges that learning and understanding a key grammatical structure doesn't mean that a student will automatically start producing this structure perfectly in writing (though wouldn't it be wonderful if this were true), students can let go of their unrealistic expectations. Instructors can stress that what students can do after learning a structure or grammar point is to become better at noticing their errors with this structure in their writing and applying specific editing strategies to correct these errors. Students can raise their own awareness in order to find specific types of errors in their own writing.

- **Survey students on their attitudes toward grammar and writing.**

Ask your students, "What do you want to learn most in your grammar class this semester?" Their answers can provide insight for both instructors and students.

- **Provide a grammar diagnostic test.**

Many grammar texts and websites provide grammar pretests and diagnostic tests meant to help students pinpoint their strengths and weaknesses. Some diagnostic tests provide graphs of a student's scores, broken down by topic (such as fragments, subject-verb agreement, and pronoun use), with links to exercises on each topic and a scorecard students and teachers can access. The results graph can be a powerful tool for students to see both their strengths and those areas they need to focus on. Taking the diagnostic test can be a first day of class activity or homework assignment, and students should be assured that the grade is for their own knowledge, not for part of a course grade. A post-test taken at the end of the course can help students measure what they've learned.

- **Help students rank errors in order of gravity.**

On the first day of class, students can be asked what particular grammatical errors they think readers notice most. Many developmental writing texts list the grammatical errors most distracting to a reader. For example, Anker (2010) lists the "four most serious errors" as: "1. Fragments, 2. Run-ons and comma splices, 3. Subject-verb agreement problems, 4. Verb problems" (p. 127). Comparing their own lists to a list such as this can help students see the difference between a serious error and a less serious one. Students can learn that by improving just the most serious errors, they can greatly improve their writing—a much more manageable and encouraging prospect.

- **Focus on errors students can learn to correct.**

Some grammatical skills (such as correct article use) are very difficult for non-native speakers of English to master. Primary emphasis should be placed on those global errors (such as subject-verb agreement or fragments) that students can learn how to self-correct.

■ **Respond to writing with coded comments.**

There are many ways to provide grammatical feedback on student writing. Ferris notes that coded comments and/or endnotes appear to work well in helping students improve their ability to self-edit (1995; 2003), particularly if provided on a rough or penultimate draft, so that students can make changes before handing in a final copy. Alternately, students could earn a small improvement in their grades if they resubmit final papers with grammatical corrections. Figure 9.1 is an overview of error marking strategies.

■ **Consider using developmental (rather than ESL) grammar textbooks.**

Many grammar textbooks designed for ESL students have international students in mind or are designed for both international and immigrant students. We have found that these texts are often more appropriate for "eye" learners of English who have more of a background in formal grammar than DI students and who are not familiar with American vocabulary, culture, and slang as much as DI students. Our students work better with *developmental* writing/grammar texts.

Goal 3: Provide Students with Easy-to-Understand Grammar Explanations and Rules

I never heard those terms before. Never.

—first-year developmental immigrant student

Challenge

Many grammar texts for native speakers or international students use a plethora of grammatical terms that developmental immigrant students, who learned English by hearing it and using it orally, are unfamiliar with. Many DI students have not had formal grammar instruction in their native language and have no basis for a discussion of grammar.

Suggested Approaches

DI students need grammatical explanations that are easy to understand along with editing guides that can be presented as charts or flowcharts. Students can also determine rules inductively, by looking at or by creating sample sentences and discovering rules for how English works.

FIGURE 9.1
Overview of Error-Marking

Error-Marking Strategies

✎ Original sentence (from an ESL student paragraph):

Study hard is very important if you wanted to go to college.

✎ Error Correction Options:

1. Error correction:

    Studying   want
    S̶t̶u̶d̶y̶ hard is very important if you w̶a̶n̶t̶e̶d̶ to go to college.

2. Error location:

    Study hard is very important if you wanted to go to college.

3. Error code:

    wf   vt
    Study hard is very important if you wanted to go to college.

4. Verbal cue:

    word form   tense
    Study hard is very important if you wanted to go to college.

5. Marginal error direction:

    Study hard is very important if you wanted to go to college.   ✓wf ✓vt

6. End comment:

    As you revise, be sure to check your verbs to see if they need to be in the past or present tense. I have underlined some examples of verb tense errors in the first part of your paragraph so that you can see what I mean.

Used with permission of Kate Kinsella (2002). Some material adapted from Ferris, D., *Treatment of Error in Second Language Student Writing,* University of Michigan Press, 2002.

■ **Emphasize that students don't need to know every grammatical term.**

Students need some basic grammar vocabulary (such as subject, verb, prepositional phrase), but focusing on every technical term takes time and focus away from working with grammar. Using more general terms (e.g. "dependent words," *to* + a verb) usually gets ideas across more easily. For example, telling students that -*ing* words and –*ing* phrases can work like nouns, like adjectives, and like parts of verbs can build awareness and understanding without a lot of complex terminology (see Folse, 2009).

■ **Provide simple charts of grammatical rules.**

Many developmental writing, editing, and grammar books provide useful charts on how to correct specific grammatical errors. Students can also work together to create their own editing charts on common issues such as how to correct run-ons and comma splices. These charts can be a useful reference or memorized as an aid for self-editing.

■ **Provide editing checklists with specific tips; encourage the use of error charts and error logs; and encourage students to make personalized grammar note cards or handbooks.**

DI students find it useful to have a checklist of grammar errors to look for and correct. These can be topics already covered in class, and students can use the checklists as a guide to editing before handing in a paper or during the last 10 minutes of an in-class timed writing assignment. Checklists include tips like reading the text backward sentence-by sentence to check for fragments or underlining subjects and verbs to check for agreement.

An error chart allows students to keep a record of the number and types of errors made on each paper throughout the semester, to track progress, and to prioritize errors. Some resources, which can be found in many learning and writing centers and in many developmental writing or editing textbooks, contain useful error charts and error logs (where students write each error on a paper, and alongside it add a correction and explanation).

Porter & vanDommelen (2005); Peters (2009); and Goen-Salter, Porter, & vanDommelen (2009) recommend that students create their own personalized grammar note cards containing simple explanations and sample sentences. Porter & vanDommelen suggest that these cards be hole-punched (a single hole in the top-left corner) and attached to a ring (such as a key ring) for easy access and review. Students can also create their own binders of easy-to-understand explanations and sample sentences for easy reference.

■ **Teach students to edit for one error at a time.**

DI students often become overwhelmed when editing their writing. By encouraging students to search for one type of error at a time, instructors can make the process less overwhelming. Students can prioritize what types of errors they should look for and correct.

■ **Provide both comprehensive feedback and selective feedback.**

Comprehensive feedback responds to all grammatical errors in a piece of writing, while selective feedback responds only to one or to a few targeted types of error. Students *want* comprehensive feedback (Leki, 1990; Ferris, 2002) on their grammatical errors, but it may make more sense logistically for instructors to sometimes comment comprehensively and focus on particular problems that are most prevalent or most global or that have been recently taught.

Goal 4: Use a Variety of Hands-On and Engaging Approaches

I hate grammar. It's so boring.

—first-year developmental immigrant student

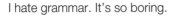

Challenge

Most students find grammar dry and boring and associate it with endless drills and workbook exercises.

Suggested Approaches

Most researchers and practitioners advocate a rich and varied approach to grammar instruction. Ellis observes that "the acquisition of the grammatical system of an L2 is a complex process and almost certainly can be assisted by a variety of approaches" (2006, p. 103). Azar recommends that when confronted with instructional choices, teachers should "do both" (2007, p.1), as a variety of approaches can be helpful to understanding and acquisition. These approaches need to work together to make the student responsible for his or her own learning. In addition, cooperative activities, manipulatives, and online tools can facilitate student interest and progress.

■ **Teach both deductive and inductive grammar.**

In deductive grammar, students are taught the rule and then apply the rule to examples. In inductive grammar, students are given or create a set of sample sentences, and students figure out the grammar rule from them. In many cases, inductive grammar can build students' interest and confidence. For example, students can list examples of fragments and complete sentences and then use the lists to determine the definition of a complete sentence. They can also use the list of fragments to determine what types of words fragments commonly start with (see Anker, 2010). These types of words can become signals to look closer at a word group to determine if it is in fact a fragment.

■ **Use both authentic and adaptive language.**

Authentic language is unaltered and comes from real-world publications or speech. It can be useful for students to edit authentic writing or find real-world examples of specific grammar points from it. Adaptive language is altered, usually to focus on a particular grammar point. Adapting texts can allow teachers to highlight particular structures. Figure 9.2 is an example of an adapted piece of student writing.

■ **Work with both sentence-level and connected discourse.**

Working at the sentence level means that each sentence is looked at in isolation. With connected discourse, students examine individual sentences that work together in a paragraph or longer piece, where coherence must be maintained. For more authentic editing practice, students should work with connected discourse whenever possible.

■ **Provide interactive and engaging activities.**

Students need multiple opportunities to work with language in order to learn grammatical rules and editing skills. Sentence strips can be used with student groups in various ways. For example, students can sort fragments and complete sentences, or correct run-on errors on the strips and then sort them according to the type of correction. In addition, many websites contain grammar exercises that provide instant feedback and explanations and track student progress. Another activity is offered by Headley (2008), who suggests providing students with blank name tags when they walk into class and asking students to write the name of a famous person on the name tag and put it on. Students must then "be" this person for the rest of the class. They can answer questions in writing as they believe this famous person would, practicing specific tenses or structures. Students enjoy this activity and are usually more willing to share their answers while in this persona.

FIGURE 9.2
Student Writing

This paragraph was taken from a student's essay and used in class to practice using the past perfect, past and present tenses.

Original student text   *(bold type added to show student's usage of verb tense)*

I **had seen** American schools on TV and on movies but when I **went** in them I **perceive** many variations, in comparison to Pakistani schools. The major one **is** that I **receive** free education in America which **is** impossible in Pakistan. In Pakistan, I **studied** for ten years but for further education I **would have to go** to college or university, but I **came** here and **had to experienced** high school. I **got** my first shock on the first day of high school when after first period a girl **came to took** me to the other class; we never **change** class in Pakistan! I **had never used** binders there, always **use** notebooks. I **had never done** any assignment on computer in Pakistan; we always **have to write down** the stuff, but in America most of the assignments **have to be** on computer. I **didn't even knew** how to print out a paper when I newly **went** to an American high school. Now I **am** a college student and the biggest advantage that I **have** of studying in America is that I **get** financial aid.

Adapted student text   *(teacher's changes and additions in italics)*

Back in Pakistan I **had seen** American schools on TV and on movies but when I **went** in them I **perceive***d* many variations, in comparison to Pakistani schools. The major one **is** that *now* I **receive** free education in America which **is** impossible in Pakistan. *Before I left* Pakistan, I *had* **studied** for ten years but for further education I **would have** *had* **to go** to college or university, but *when I was 15* I **came** here and ~~**had to**~~ **experienced** high school. I **got** my first shock on the first day of high school when after first period a girl **came to** *take* me to the other class; we *had* **never changed** class in Pakistan! I **had never used** binders there*; I had* **always used** notebooks. I **had never done** any assignment on computer in Pakistan; we *had* **always** *written* **down** the stuff, but in America most of the assignments **have to be** on computer. I **didn't even** *know* how to print out a paper when I newly **went** to an American high school. Now I **am** a college student and the biggest advantage that I **have** of studying in America is that I **get** financial aid.

Student text to use in class
Directions- Highlight according to tense: past perfect=yellow, past= blue, present tense= pink
        Time expressions are underlined to give you clues.

Back in Pakistan I **had seen** American schools on TV and on movies but <u>when I **went** in them</u> I **perceived** many variations, in comparison to Pakistani schools. The major one **is** that <u>now</u> I **receive** free education in America which **is** impossible in Pakistan. Before I left Pakistan, I **had studied** for ten years but for further education I **would have had to go** to college or university, but <u>when I was 15</u> I **came** here and **experienced** high school. I **got** my first shock <u>on the first day of high school when after first period</u> a girl **came to take** me to the other class; we **had never changed** class <u>in Pakistan!</u> I **had never used** binders there; I **had always used** notebooks. I **had never done** any assignment on computer <u>in Pakistan</u>; we **had always written down** the stuff, but <u>in America</u> most of the assignments **have to be** on computer. I **didn't even know** how to print out a paper <u>when I newly **went** to an American high school</u>. <u>Now</u> I **am** a college student and the biggest advantage that I **have** of studying in America is that I **get** financial aid.

Adapted from Peters, 2009. Used with permission of Jennifer Peters.

Goal 5: Teach Meaning as Well as Grammar

I only get to see them **until** the weekends come and that makes me stay at home for most days of the weeks.

My father is a mechanical engineer. **Otherwise**, he is well respected and can answer any question.

—first-year developmental immigrant student's writing

Challenge

Using logical connectors and hedging words correctly requires understanding of grammatical usage and slight differences in meaning between expressions. Often DI students do not understand the meaning of logical connectors, causing them to create errors in writing and to misunderstand or not comprehend what they read. In addition, DI students who do not use hedging words (perhaps because such words are not needed in their native language or they do not understand the subtle difference in meaning sentences without them convey) cannot produce strong argumentative essays.

Suggested Approaches

DI students need to be explicitly taught the meaning and usage of transition and hedging words and practice using them and editing for them in their own writing.

■ **Teach the meaning and use of logical connectors.**

When teaching the use of logical connectors (such as prepositions, dependent words [which begin dependent clauses], and transition words), instructors should emphasize the meaning and subtle differences between these words. The instructor and students should discuss possible choices that would logically link two given sentences, and students should practice using these logical connectors correctly in their own writing. (Some dependent words are particularly difficult for DI students, including *although, even though, unless, so,* and *so that.*) In addition, students need to know how these connectors are used: Are they followed by a clause or a noun? Can they introduce a sentence or are they dependent, creating a fragment if not connected to another sentence?

■ **Teach the meaning and use of hedging words.**

The use of hedging words (such as *usually, almost always, many,* or *most*) is critical in American academic writing, yet it is not emphasized in many other cultures. A writer who does not use hedging words in a persuasive or argumentative essay runs the risk of sounding too absolute, giving the opposition good reason to poke holes in his argument. "Hedging" words are used to soften a claim and make it less absolute. DI students should learn the importance of hedging words (a class debate on a controversial topic is a useful way to teach the importance of hedging) and practice using them.

If developmental immigrant students are taught to notice and prioritize their grammatical errors and are given specific strategies to correct them, they can become better editors of and gain more control over their own writing.

Additional Useful Websites

- **Exercise Central**
  www.bedfordstmartins.com/exercisecentral
  Free grammar diagnostics and exercises tailored to students' results.

- **Comfit**
  www.comfit.com
  Online language arts exercises and tutorials. Free 14-day trial; then you must pay a fee. Institutional rates available.

- **Big Dog's Guide to Grammar by Scott Foll**
  www.aliscot.com/bigdog
  Student-friendly explanations and online quizzes.

- **Grammar Bytes**
  www.chompchomp.com
  Online grammar exercises and handouts.

- **D'Youville College Learning Center Online Writing Lab**
  http://depts.dyc.edu/learningcenter/owl/
  Explanations and online exercises for many grammar points.

- **Quia Web**
  www.quia.com
  Searchable index of games and quizzes made by teachers from around the world.

Appendixes

Appendix 2a: Description of Courses in the American Studies Cluster

The American Studies Cluster—Course Descriptions

The 30-Hour Summer Program

The 30-Hour Program is a student-developed and student-conducted program for <u>all</u> at-risk students (not just DI students) offered during the summer prior to freshman year. The 30-Hour Program is not meant to replace or to "teach" freshman courses; it is meant to emphasize what is important to prepare students for these courses: organizing time; following directions; understanding assignments; and mastering math, grammar, and writing skills. Such skills are expected of all students in higher education. The summer program entails 30 hours of peer tutoring in writing, math, reading, and study skills. The peer tutors let the incoming students know what they will need to do in college, they serve as models for the students, they begin friendships with the students, and they introduce students to the Learning Center, which becomes these students' "home" or safe haven on campus. Enrolled students establish their own schedules but sign a contract to complete all required work prior to the beginning of the fall semester. Following are the skills covered:

30-Hour Summer Program Skills

<u>Writing Skills</u>

   *Completion of a diagnostic essay—to identify basic writing skill needs

   *Completion of three paragraphs using the writing process and structure expected in developmental English classes

   *Introduction to word processing

   *Grammar and punctuation assessment and remediation

   *Development of personalized proofreading checklist

   *Use of a thesaurus for vocabulary development

Math Skills

   *Completion of pre-math diagnostic test to identify weaknesses and strengths

   *Individual instruction to improve skills as indicated on the diagnostic test

   *Preparation for a specific fall math course

   *Completion of post math diagnostic test

Reading Skills

   *List of recommended classics to read during the summer

   *Informal small group discussion of short stories and poems

   *Practice in reading for the main idea

Strategies and Techniques for College Success

   *Completion and discussion of learning style inventory

   *Setting up of long- and short-term goals

   *"Coping with Freshman Year" discussion

   *Introduction to basic library research skills

   *Familiarization with University computer system network

Introduction to College Summer Program

The Introduction to College Program, which meets the week prior to the start of the fall semester, is a program designed to introduce incoming American Studies Cluster students to campus resources and to provide more intensive instruction on English language skills, study skills, organizational skills, time management, and money management. Students meet with the Director of Academic Affairs, the Chancellor, and several other key staff people, as well as with several of the faculty that they will have as instructors during the first semester. The class is based on hands-on activities—analyzing syllabi, for example—in order to expose the students to the reality of academia and its educational expectations and to help change any misconceptions regarding course work and the college experience.

Description of Core Cluster Courses (Fall Semester)

Each of the following courses can be adopted by or adapted to any college or university program:

American Studies

The centerpiece of the ASC is the American Studies course, a course that focuses on American history and culture, and which provides the impetus for the other courses in the cluster. In other words, the material covered in the American Studies course is the same material that drives the grammar, composition, reading skills, and seminar courses. For example, one unit in the American Studies course focuses on government and politics, which is discussed at length in the American Studies class, from both American and cross-cultural perspectives. The students will then continue the "discussions" outside of class, writing and responding to a political issue in preparation for an in-class debate and PowerPoint presentation. In conjunction with these discussions, students in the composition class will write a persuasive essay, using the information and analysis they've learned in American Studies and the Reading class. In the grammar course the students will focus on the sentence structure and editing of their essay, and in the reading course they will read and discuss current articles about politics and government. Enriching and reinforcing these course assignments is a lecture on politics and/or government (war in Iraq, for example) given by a political science professor, which is then followed by a seminar discussion, where key points from the lecture are highlighted and clarified. Other topics/lectures include Religion, Business, Health and Sports, Immigration and Racial Issues, Education, and Family Life. The continual reinforcement of material allows students the time and support needed to understand fully the material being taught. During the second semester this reinforcement continues in other ways. For example, we encourage students to participate in an undergraduate research project, which is presented to the entire campus community at the annual Undergraduate Research Symposium. Students who present their research become much more confident and connected to the campus community.

The American Studies course not only provides content, but it also provides opportunities to introduce the students to the higher education system. Students gain a sense of the university—what other courses entail and how the disciplines are connected. The desired outcome is that students have a sense of what it means to be "American" in the United States, and how they, as bicultural students, can navigate their way between two cultures.

First-Year Seminar

First-Year Seminar (FYS), which is integrated into a content course on our campus, is a course required of all first-year students. The course is designed to provide freshman students with skills they need for academic survival, and these skills are seamlessly woven within the context of the American Studies course as part of the American Studies Cluster (FYS is also a non-credit course on our campus, so the grade assigned to the content course includes the FYS component). The focus of the FYS within the ASC is to develop and improve communication, research, and critical-thinking and computer literacy skills (during scheduled American Studies class sessions). Perhaps an even more important component of the first-year seminar is that it allows students to synthesize and verbalize what they're experiencing on campus, as it provides them with the opportunity to go through a process of "growth and reflection" (Goldschmidt

& Ziemba, 2001) where they can begin to gain perspective on their lives and how they fit in, and sometimes don't fit in, and at other times, don't want to fit in to the American culture. In other words, this forum enables them to establish their "very sense of self" (Harklau, 2000).

College Reading and Study Skills

The College Reading and Study Skills course is intended to develop effective strategies for reading and interpreting college texts and to assist students in developing effective study skills. The strategies taught are applied to reading assignments and other assignments in the American Studies course. Although this course serves as an adjunct course to American Studies in that it provides broader background knowledge for the course, the students are also prepared for subsequent college courses. Additional readings, which are topically related, are used to supplement the American Studies course and to give students experience with a variety of texts typical of what they will encounter in the various disciplines. Students learn vocabulary related to a reading, strategies to assist them in reading and understanding the text, and study skills that help them prepare for class, exams and projects. The course also provides them with opportunities to develop speaking skills, both formal and informal. The instructor of this course meets regularly with the instructor of the American Studies course to develop continuity and support between the two courses.

Basic Writing

Writing, for most of these students, presents the greatest challenge. The course provides intensive instruction and practice in writing sentences and paragraphs, with particular attention to the use of graphic organizers, and discussion and revision of multiple drafts. The course moves from paragraph to essay-level writing and focuses on organization, development, and revision and editing strategies so they can perform well in various writing tasks within the university (and beyond) and so that their writing proficiency is commensurate with their oral proficiency. Since the university has a standardized composition program, in which students are taught the same essay techniques (compare/contrast, illustration, etc.), the students tend not to feel stigmatized. They are writing the same types of essays as other freshman students, only their instructor is ESL trained.

English Grammar (English Language Analysis)

The grammar course, which works in tandem with the basic writing course, focuses on grammatical problems encountered in the students' writing. Because the students are lacking in knowledge about grammatical forms or usage, the course encourages students to recognize why and when certain forms are used in a sentence as well as why and when they are not. Shih (1998) has found that misconceptions about syntactic structures are a major reason why writers miss finding sentence-level errors. Students learn to identify grammatical problems in their writing (from the basic writing course) and try to eliminate them so that they may communicate their ideas more effectively.

One-on-One Writing Tutorial

Students meet for a half hour once a week in the learning center (many drop in for a second half hour each week), always with the same instructor/tutor, where they receive help with writing and grammar (as well as 1 credit). Typically the learning center instructor will help a student with the planning and revising stages of the writing process as well as focusing on grammatical problems the student might be encountering. The learning center instructor discusses each student's progress with the basic writing instructor throughout the semester.

One-on-One Math Tutorial (If Needed)

The math tutorial provides weekly individualized instruction in the campus Learning Center for students to support the math course into which they are placed.

Description of Expansion Courses: (Spring Semester)

College Rhetoric and Composition

Students write longer, more developed essays, often in response to class readings or class discussions. Focus is on reading-writing connections and sound argument as students move beyond the 5–6 paragraph essay.

One-on-One Writing Tutorial

Tutorial instruction in composition and rhetoric for students currently enrolled in either English course takes place in the campus learning center. Again, this is a 1 credit course as described for the first semester.

College Reading and Study Skills II

This course entails a higher level of comprehension, vocabulary, and study skills incorporated into content area reading. Activities and instruction build upon the first semester reading and study skills course. Students often work directly with material from content courses they are currently taking in order to apply strategies learned.

Comparative Literature and Film

In this course, students are taught with a strong reading-writing focus as they respond critically to essays, short stories, and films by a variety of writers and film makers from throughout the world, examining films from multiple perspectives and positions. Students develop global literacy as they gain cultural knowledge and uncover universal themes.

Enrichment Courses and Opportunities: Adult Literacy and Service Learning

This is a six-credit independent study course in which all enrolled students (both DI students and traditional students) attend classes and provide 40 hours of tutoring while being trained in teaching adult literacy. Because the students actually teach English, they gain a better understanding of the English language: Some of the weakest students have made the most gains. The students are also introduced to issues related to illiteracy. The "students" being taught are non-native English speaking adults (over the age of 18).

Community Service

We also offer a separate Community Service course for 1–3 credits, depending on the number of hours of service provided by the students. This course does not have the research paper component attached to it, but it does include the reflective component.

Undergraduate Research

Both DI students and other immigrant students at our campus are in a unique position to share a wide variety of cultural traditions. In the last several years, our campus has benefited from cross-cultural exhibitions by all of our immigrant students. In addition, several of our immigrant students have received undergraduate research grants to conduct research and to share this research at our on-campus research exhibition. These research opportunities foster pride in as well as recognition of the diverse contributions of our immigrant students. In addition, several of our immigrant students have had essays from their first year writing courses published in university-wide (and state-wide) writing journals. Finally, all of our DI students have their best (self-selected) essays from their Freshman Composition course in the spring semester published in an in-house booklet.

Learning Center Workshops and Seminars (ongoing)

The Learning Center holds a variety of workshops, for all students on campus, twice monthly throughout the semester to provide additional support to the students. Instructors can recommend or required attendance at a workshop. Workshops can also be taught (in the classroom) in the event that an instructor would otherwise have to cancel class. The workshops include:

1. Using time effectively

2. Taking class notes

3. Getting organized for quizzes and tests

4. Reading efficiently and effectively

5. Using your memory effectively

6. Taking tests and exams

7. Last minute exam preparation

8. Managing stress

Appendix 4a: Examining a Syllabus

Name _____

DIRECTIONS: Choose a syllabus. Carefully examine it, the textbook for the course, and the textbook's website (if applicable) in order to answer the following.

READING	
How many pages will you be required to read EACH WEEK?	
How many vocabulary words must you learn each week? (HINT: Look at the end of each chapter in the textbook.)	
TESTS	
How many tests or exams do students take in the class?	
How many chapters does each test or exam cover?	
What percentage of the final grade is each test or exam?	

OTHER ASSIGNMENTS AND EXPECTATIONS What other assignments or requirements factor into the grade? What percent of the grade are they? Are they described in detail in the syllabus?	
ADDITIONAL RESOURCES Does your textbook have a companion website (check the back cover or introduction of the textbook)? If so, what does the site provide? Does the syllabus suggest ways of studying for the course? If so, what are the suggestions?	
WRITING What kind of writing is required in the class? How much of your grade depends on written work?	
COURSE POLICIES What is the professor's policy on . . . •late assignments? •absences? •being late to class? •make-up tests? •communicating with students? •academic integrity?	

Appendix 4b: Entrance Survey

ENTRANCE SURVEY

Rate your feelings from 1–5, considering the following scale:

1—Very Negative   2—Negative   3—Neutral   4—Positive   5—Very Positive

1. How do you feel about attending college?   1 2 3 4 5

2. How do you feel about entering this campus?   1 2 3 4 5

3. How do you feel about starting this summer program?   1 2 3 4 5

4. How do you feel when you are doing math?   1 2 3 4 5

5. How do you feel about reading in general?   1 2 3 4 5

6. How do you feel when you are given a reading assignment?   1 2 3 4 5

7. How do you feel when you are told to write in class?   1 2 3 4 5

8. How do you feel about being tutored?   1 2 3 4 5

9. If you are having trouble with a subject, how do you feel   1 2 3 4 5
   about asking for extra help?

10. How do you feel about studying?   1 2 3 4 5

11. How do you feel about learning?   1 2 3 4 5

12. How do you feel about your ability to manage your time?   1 2 3 4 5

13. How do you feel about getting involved in extracurricular   1 2 3 4 5
    activities at this campus?

14. How do you feel about your ability to handle the difficulty 1 2 3 4 5
    of the work at this campus?

15. How do you feel about your ability to handle the workload   1 2 3 4 5
    at this campus?

Other Comments: Please feel free to elaborate on your answers.

Appendix 8a: First Day of Class Survey

Name _____

DIRECTIONS: Please answer the following questions so that I may get to know you better.

- What classes are you taking this semester?

- What do you LIKE about writing?

- In writing, what do you do well?

- What do you HATE about writing?

- In writing, what is difficult for you?

- What do you hope we learn/do in class this semester?

- What do you hope we DON'T learn/do in class this semester?

On the back of your paper, write a paragraph introducing yourself to the class.

Appendix 8b: Illustrative Paragraph Graphic Organizer Choices

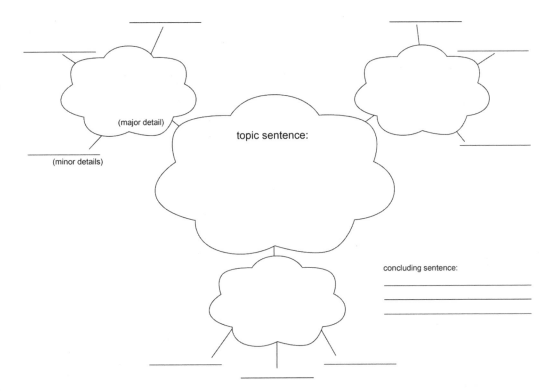

(major detail)

(minor details)

topic sentence:

concluding sentence:

topic sentence

(major detail)

(minor detail)

concluding sentence

topic sentence: _____
_____

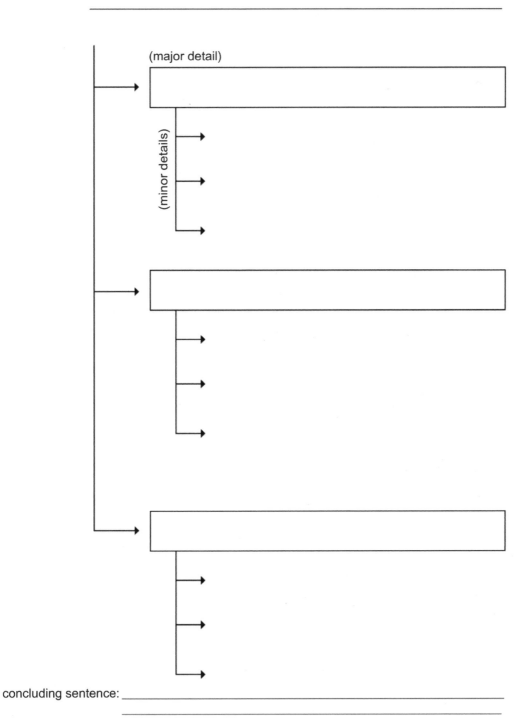

(major detail)

(minor details)

concluding sentence: _____
_____

topic sentence: _____

_____

A. _____ (major detail)

   1. _____ (minor detail)

   2. _____

   3. _____

B. _____

   1. _____

   2. _____

   3. _____

C. _____

   1. _____

   2. _____

   3. _____

concluding sentence: _____

_____

Appendix 8c: Reflecting on Your Essay

Name _____

Reflecting on your essay (for use with a final draft)

1. What do you like best about your essay?

2. What was easiest for you in writing this essay?

3. What was most difficult for you in writing this essay? How (specifically) did you attempt to solve this problem?

4. What are 2–3 things you REVISED for in this essay?
   (organization + details)

5. What are 2–3 specific grammatical issues you EDITED for in this essay?

6. What specific skills or strategies do you want to work on next time?

Appendix 8d: End-of-Semester Reflection

Name _____

- What is your favorite piece of writing from this semester?

- Why is it your favorite?

- What other things do you like about your writing from this semester? Why?

- What do you think has improved the most about your writing this semester? Explain.

- What has improved the most about your grammar this semester? Explain.

- What writing skills do you want to continue to work on?

- What grammar points do you still want to work on?

- Did you develop any new writing strategies this semester? What worked well for you as you went through the process of writing a paper?

- What didn't work well as you went through the writing process this semester? What would you change about your work this semester if you could?

- What are your thoughts about taking an English course next semester or in the future?

Appendix 8e: English Final Writing Assignment

Name _____

Final Draft due _____

This semester we have read about and discussed many writers' processes and views on writing. For this assignment, you need to share **your own views on writing** in a clear and thoughtful way.

Write an **essay of at least 2 ½ pages** that expresses your own current views on writing. You can approach this assignment in many ways. Some possibilities include

- explaining your own writing process and how it benefits you
- tracing your history of writing (from childhood to the present or from your arrival in America to the present)
- arguing how writing should be taught in high school (or in college) and why
- comparing how you write in a native language to how you write in English
- tracing your history of your attitudes toward writing
- tracing how you have used writing in the past and how you will use it in the future
- responding to the question posed to Amy Tan: "Why are there so few Asian-American writers?" (You could write about a different ethnic group if you choose, and you could disagree with the statement if you choose or offer a solution to this problem.)
- offering advice on writing to an incoming freshman
- explaining what you will teach your own children someday about writing
- explaining what you have learned about yourself through your writing this semester

- evaluating your own writing this past semester and how it has affected you
- explaining how thinking and writing are related for you
- explaining what the relationship between reading and writing is for you
- comparing writing in your native country with writing in the United States
- discussing writing as a process of discovery
- defining "writing" or "writer" in a personal way
- responding to a quotation (or quotations) about writing.
  Some can be found here: http://www.quotegarden.com/writing.html or
  http://thinkexist.com/quotations/writing/

You may use one, some, or none of the above writing prompts as a guide. I do not simply want an essay that says that planning ahead and using the Learning Center helps you write (though you can include that idea if you wish). Instead, I'm looking for **your attitudes toward writing, the effect writing has on you, your thoughts about the importance or power of writing, and/or how writing has affected you in a personal way. Basically this is a paper about YOU and WRITING.**

Enjoy this essay—you've grown so much this year!

References

Allen, R. (2000). Before it's too late: Giving reading a last chance. *Curriculum Update*, 1–3, 6–8.

Allison, H. (2009). High school academic literacy instruction and the transition to college writing. In M. Roberge, M. Siegal, & L. Harklau (Eds.), *Generation 1.5 in college composition: Teaching academic writing to U.S.-educated learners of ESL* (pp. 75–90). New York: Routledge.

Anker, S. (2010). *Real Skills with Readings: Sentences and paragraphs for college, work, and everyday life.* 2nd ed. New York: Bedford/St. Martin's.

Ashworth, P., & Bannister, P. (1997). Guilty in whose eyes?: University students' preceptions of cheating and plagiarism in academic work and assessment. *Studies in Higher Education, 22*(2), 187–203.

Azar, B. (2007). Grammar-based teaching: A practitioner's perspective. *TESL-EJ, 11*(2), 1–12.

Benesch, S. (1988). Ending remediation: Linking ESL and content in higher education. Paper presented at TESOL. Washington, DC.

Bettinger, E.P., & Long, B.T. (2009). Addressing the needs of under-prepared college students: Does college remediation work? *The Journal of Human Resources, 44*(3), 736–771.

Blanton, L. (1992). A holistic approach to college ESL: Integrating language and content. *ELT Journal, 46*(3), 285–293.

Blanton, L. (1999). Classroom instruction and language minority students: On teaching to "smarter" readers and writers." In L. Harklau, K.M. Losey, & M. Siegal (Eds.), *Generation 1.5 meets college composition* (pp. 119–142). Mahwah, NJ: Lawrence Erlbaum.

Bourdieu, P. (1998). *Practical reason: On the theory of action.* Palo Alto, CA: Stanford University Press.

Boylan, H. R. (2001). Making the case for developmental education. *Research in Developmental Education, 12*(2), 1–4.

Brooks-Terry, M. (1988). Tracing the disadvantages of first-generation college students: An application of Sussman's option sequence model. In S. Steinmetz (Ed.), *Family and support systems across the life span* (pp. 121–134). New York: Plenum.

Brown, C. (2004). Content-based ESL curriculum and academic language proficiency. *The Internet TESL Journal*, February.

Brown, C. F. (2009). Personal interview, November.

Brown, C. L., Park, Y., Jeong, E., & Staples, A. T. (2006). Korean perspectives: Content-based ESL through thematic units. *TNTESOL Newsletter, 27*(2–3), 5 and 9–10.

Byrd, K. L., & MacDonald, G. (2005). Defining college readiness from the inside out: First-generation college student perspectives. *Community College Review, 33*(1), 22–37.

Cantoni-Harvey, G. (1987). *Content-area language instruction: Approaches and strategies.* Reading, MA: Addison-Wesley.

Capple L., & Curtis A. (2000). Content-based instruction in Hong Kong, Student responses to film. *System, 28,* 419–433.

Casazza, M.E. (1999). Who are we and where did we come from? *Journal of Developmental Education, 23*(1), 2–7.

Chamot, A. U. (2004). Issues in language learning strategy research and teaching. *Electronic Journal of Foreign Language Teaching, 1*(1), 14–26.

Chamot, A.U., & O'Malley, J.M. (1994). *The CALLA handbook: Implementing cognitive academic language learning approach.* New York: Longman.

Chute, E. (2008). Students face a long list of obstacles on the way to college degree. *Pittsburgh Post-Gazette,* August 31.

Clydesdale, T. (2007). *The first year out: Understanding American teens after high school.* Chicago: University of Chicago Press.

Collier, P. J., & Morgan, D.L. (2007). "Is that paper really due today?": Differences in first-generation and traditional college students' understandings of faculty expectations. *Higher Education, 55,* 425–446.

Conley, D. (2005). *College knowledge: What it really takes for students to succeed and what we can do to get them ready.* San Francisco: Jossey-Bass.

Conley, D. (2007). Toward a more comprehensive conception of college readiness. Prepared for the Bill & Melinda Gates Foundation, March.

Cooperative Institutional Research Program. (2005). The 2003 CIRP Freshman survey data. From http://adminplan.crown.northwestern.edu/ir/cirp/all.pdf

Coxhead, A. (1998). An academic word list (English Language Institute Occasional Publication No. 18). Wellington, New Zealand: Victoria University of Wellington.

Coxhead, A. (2000). A new academic word list. *TESOL Quarterly, 34*(2), 213–238.

Crosby, C. (2007). *The academic literacies experiences of Generation 1.5 learners: How three Generation 1.5 learners negotiated various academic literacies contexts in their first year of university study.* Doctoral dissertation. Ohio State University.

Crosby, C. (2009). Academic reading and writing difficulties and strategic knowledge of Generation 1.5 learners. In M. Roberge, M. Siegal, & L. Harklau (Eds.), *Generation 1.5 in college composition: Teaching academic writing to U.S.-educated learners of ESL.* New York: Routledge.

Cummins, J. (1979). Cognitive/academic language proficiency, linguistic interdependence, the optimum age question and some other matters. *Working Papers on Bilingualism, 19,* 121–129.

Cummins, J. (1981). Four misconceptions about language proficiency in bilingual education. *NABE Journal, 5*(3), 31–45.

D'Angelo-Long, M. (2004). Teach your children well: The high school research experience. In *The plagiarism plague: A resource guide and CD-ROM tutorial for educators and librarians* (pp. 71–78). New York: Neal-Schuman.

Danico, M. Y. (2004). *The 1.5 generation: Becoming Korean American in Hawai'i.* Westport, CT: Greenwood Press.

Davies, T.G., Safarik, L., & Banning, J.H. (2003). The deficit portrayal of underrepresented population on community college campuses: A cross case analysis. *Community College Journal of Research and Practice, 27,* 843–858.

Davis, M., & Hult, R. (1997). Effects of writing summaries as a generative learning activity during notetaking. *Teaching of Psychology, 24,* 47–49.

de Szendeffy, J. (2005). *A practical guide to using computers in language teaching.* Ann Arbor: University of Michigan Press.

Dickson, S. V., Chard, D. J., & Simmons, D. C. (1993). An integrated reading/writing curriculum: A focus on scaffolding. *LD Forum, 18*(4), 12–16.

Dillon, J. (2007). Widening the circle: Adapting literature circles for the college level developmental reading class. *Research & Teaching in Education, 24*(1), 83–86.

Disbro, W. (1996). *100 things every college student ought to know.* Williamsville, NY: Cambridge Stratford Study Skills Institute.

Duenas, M. (2004). A description of prototype models for content-based language instruction in higher education. *International Journal of English Studies, 4*(1), 73–96.

Dunn, R., & Dunn, K. (1993). *Teaching secondary students through their individual learning styles.* Boston: Allyn & Bacon.

Dunn, R., & Griggs, S. A. (Eds). (2000). *Practical approaches to using learning styles in higher education.* Westpoint, CT: Bergin & Garvey.

Dunn, R., Honigsfeld, A., & Doolan, L. S. (2009). Impact of learning-style instructional strategies on students' achievement and attitudes: Perceptions of educators in diverse institutions. *The Clearing House, 82*(3), 135–140.

Durst, R.K. (1999). *Collision course: Conflict, negotiation, and learning in college composition.* Urbana, IL: National Council of Teachers of English.

Dzubak, C. (2007). What skills and whose standards: Why are students underprepared? The Facilitating Newsletter of the Association of the Tutoring Profession. Nashville.

Edwards, K. E., & McKelfresh, D. A. (2002). The impact of a residential college on students' academic success and persistence. *Journal of College Student Development, 43,* 395–401.

Ellis, R. (2006). Current issues in the teaching of grammar: An SLA perspective. *TESOL Quarterly, 40,* 83–107.

Enright, G. (1997). LAC, LRC, and developmental education: An orientation for the beginning learning center professional. In S. Mioduski & G. Enright (Eds.), *Proceedings for the 15th and 16th annual institutes for learning assistance professionals: 1994 and 1995.* Tucson: University Learning Center, University of Arizona.

Erikson, Erik H. (1950). *Childhood and society.* New York: Norton.

Ferris, D. (1995). Student reaction to teacher response in multi-draft composition classrooms. *TESOL Quarterly, 29*(1), 33–41.

Ferris, D. (2002). *Treatment of error in second language student writing.* Ann Arbor: University of Michigan Press.

Ferris, D. (2003). *Response to student writing: Implications for second language students.* Mahwah, NJ: Lawrence Erlbaum.

Ferris, D. R., & Hedgcock, J. (2005). *Teaching ESL composition: Purpose, process, and practice,* 2nd ed. Mahwah, NJ: Lawrence Earlbaum.

Fleming, N. (2001). VARK: A guide to learning styles. www.vark-learn.com

Folse, K. (2004). *Vocabulary myths: Applying second language research to classroom teaching.* Ann Arbor: University of Michigan Press.

Folse, K. (2009). *Keys to teaching grammar to English language learners: A practical handbook.* Ann Arbor: University of Michigan Press.

Forrest, S. N. (2006). Three foci of an effective high school Generation 1.5 literacy program. *Journal of Adolescent & Adult Literacy, 50*(2), 106–112.

Frodesen, J. (2001). Balancing fluency and accuracy in academic language instruction for mainstreamed L2 writers. Paper presented at the 35th TESOL Convention, St. Louis, MO.

Gibbs, L.L. (1994). Analysis of developmental mathematics programs in Texas which are successful with Black and Hispanic students. *Dissertation Abstracts International, 55*(06), 1457A (UMI No. 9428521).

Goen, S., Porter, P., Swanson, D., & vanDommelen, D. (2001). Working with generation 1.5 teachers and learners. 35th TESOL Convention, St. Louis, MO.

Goen-Salter, S., Porter, P., & vanDommelen, D. (2009). Working with generation 1.5: Pedagological principles and practices. In M. Roberge, M. Siegal, & L. Harklau (Eds.), *Generation 1.5 in college composition: Teaching academic writing to U.S.-educated learners of ESL* (pp. 235–259). New York: Routledge.

Goldschmidt, M., & Ziemba, C. (2003). Course clustering: A comprehensive program for Generation 1.5. *College ESL, 10*(1–2), 22–36.

Goldschmidt, M., Notzold, N., & Ziemba-Miller, C. (2003). ESL student transition to college: The 30-hour program. *Journal of Developmental Education, 12*(2), 71–79.

Goldschmidt, M., & Ousey, D. (2006). Jump start to resolving developmental immigrant students' misconceptions about college. *Research & Teaching in Developmental Education, 22*(2), 16–30.

Goldschmidt, M., & Seifried, T. (2008). Mismatched expectations among developmental ESL students in higher education. *Research & Teaching in Developmental Education, 24*(2), 27–39.

Grabe, W. (2009). *Reading in a second language: Moving from theory to practice.* Cambridge, U.K.: Cambridge University Press.

Greene, J.P., & Forster, G. (2003). *Public high school graduation and college readiness rates in the United States.* Manhattan Institute for Policy Research.

Greenleaf, C., Cziko, C., & Mueller, F.L. (2001). Apprenticing adolescent readers to academic literacy. *Harvard Educational Review, 71*(1), 79–129.

Hamrick, F.A., Evans, N.J., & Schuh, J.H. (2002). *Foundations of student affairs practice.* San Francisco: Jossey-Bass.

Harklau, L. (1998). Newcomers in U.S. higher education: Questions of access and Equity. *Educational Policy, 12*, 634–658.

Harklau, L. (2000). From the "good kids" to the "worst": Representations of English language learners across educational settings. *TESOL Quarterly, 34*, 35–67.

Harklau, L. (2003). Representational practices and multi-modal communication in U.S. high schools: Implications for adolescent immigrants. In R. Bayley & S. R. Schecter (Eds.), *Language socialization in bilingual and multilingual societies* (pp. 83–97). New York: Multilingual Matters.

Harklau, L., Losey, K. M., & Siegal, M. (1999). *Generation 1.5 meets college composition: Issues in teaching writing to U.S.-educated learners of ESL.* Mahwah, NJ: Lawrence Erlbaum.

Headley, E. (2008). Salt, pepper, and hot sauce: Quick ways to enhance the flavor of a lesson. Presentation at the Fall 2008 PennTESOL-East Conference. Penn State Abington. November 1.

Hedgcock, J.S., & Ferris, D.R. (2009). *Teaching readers of English: Students, texts, and contexts.* New York: Routledge.

Heller, R., & Greenleaf, C. (2007). *Literacy instruction in the content areas. The alliance for excellent education.* Washington, DC.

Henry, M. (2004). Communicating honesty: Building on the student-teacher relationship. In V. Bowman (Ed.), *The Plagiarism Plague* (pp. 79–94). New York: Neal-Shuman.

Hinkel, E. (2005). *Handbook of research in second language teaching and learning.* Mahwah, NJ: Lawrence Erlbaum.

Hirvela, A. (2004). *Connecting reading and writing in second language writing instruction.* Ann Arbor: University of Michigan Press.

Hogan, K., & Pressley, M. (1997). *Scaffolding student learning: Instructional approaches & issues.* Cambridge, MA: Brookline Books, Inc.

Holten, C. (1997). Literature: A quintessential content. In M.A. Snow & D.M. Brinton (Eds.), *The Content-Based Classroom: Perspectives on Integrating Language and Content* (pp. 377–387). White Plains, NY: Addison-Wesley Longman.

Howard, P. M. (1995). Plagiarisms, authorship, and the academic death penalty. *College English, 57*(7), 788–806.

Hoye, M. (1988). *The effects of summary writing on the reading comprehension of American and ESL university freshmen.* Doctoral dissertation. University of Texas at Austin.

Hyland, F. (2001). Dealing with plagiarism while giving feedback. *ELT Journal, 55*(4), 375–381.

Jenson, E. (2003). *Student Success Secrets*, 5th ed. New York: Barron's.

Kaplan, R. (1966). Cultural thought patterns in intercultural education. *Language Learning, 16*(1), 1–20.

Kasper, L.F. (1994). Improved reading performance for ESL students through academic course pairing. *Journal of Reading, 37*, 376–384.

Kasper, L.F. (1995). Using discipline-based texts to boost college ESL reading instruction. *Journal of Adolescent & Adult Literacy, 39*(4), 298–306.

Kasper, L.F. (1997). The impact of content-based instructional programs on the academic progress of ESL students. *English for Specific Purposes, 16*(4), 309–320.

Kasper, L.F. (1998). Meeting ESL students' academic needs through discipline-based instructional programs. In T. Smoke (Ed.), *Adult ESL: Politics, pedagogy, and participation in classroom and community programs* (pp. 147–157). Hillsdale, NJ: Lawrence Erlbaum.

Kasper, L.F. (2000). *Content-based college ESL instruction.* Mahwah, NJ: Lawrence Erlbaum.

Kaspar, L. F., Babbitt, M., Mlynarczyk, R. W., Brinton, D. M., Rosenthal, J. W., Master, P., Myers, S. A., Egbert, J., Tillyer, D. A., & Wood, L. S. (2000). *Content-based college ESL instruction.* Mahwah, NJ: Lawrence Erlbaum.

Kaur, J., & Hegelheimer, V. (2005). ESL students' use of concordance in the transfer of academic word knowledge: An exploratory study. *Computer Assisted Language Learning, 18*(4), 287–310.

Keeling, S. (2003). Advising the millennial generation. *NACADA Journal, 23*(1&2), 30–36.

Keene, E., & Zimmerman, S. (1997). *Mosaic of thought.* Portsmouth, NH: Heinemann.

Kelly, W. J., & Lawton, D.L. (2006). *Odyssey: From paragraph to essay*, 4th ed. New York: Longman.

Kiang, P. N. (1992). Issues of curriculum and community for first-generation Asian Americans in college. In L. S. Zwerling & H. B. London (Eds.), *First-generation students: Confronting the cultural issues* (pp. 97–112). San Francisco: Jossey-Bass.

Kimmel, I., & Davis, J. R. (1996). Moving to the center: Students' strategies for college survival. *Research & Teaching in Developmental Education, 12*(2), 71–79.

King, N. (2004). Advising underprepared students. Presentation: NACADA Summer Institute on Advising. Manhattan, KS.

Kinsella, Kate. (2002). Error making strategies, p. 97. www.oaklandwrites.org/writing-proc.html Adapted from D. R. Ferris, *Treatment of error in second language student writing.* Ann Arbor: University of Michigan Press.

Kissner, E. (2006). *Summarizing, paraphrasing and retelling: Skills for better reading, writing, and test taking.* Portsmouth, NH: Heinemann.

Krashen, S. (1981a). *Beyond language acquisition and second language learning.* Oxford: Pergamon Press.

Krashen, S. (1981b). *Principles and practice in second language acquisition.* English Language Teaching series. London: Prentice-Hall International (UK) Ltd.

Krashen, S. (1985). *The input hypothesis: Issues and implications.* New York: Longman.

Kuhn, M., & Stahl, S. (1998). Teaching students to learn word meanings from context: A synthesis and some questions. *Journal of Literary Research, 30,* 119–138.

Lackie, R. J., & D'Angelo-Long, M. (2004). It's a small world?: Cross cultural perspectives and ESL considerations. In V. Bowman (Ed.), *The plagiarism plague: A resource guide and CD-ROM tutorial for educators and librarians* (pp. 35–48). New York: Neal-Shuman.

Lang, J.M. (2008). The myth of first-year enlightenment. *Chronicle of Higher Education, 54* (Issue 21), C1.

Leki, I. (1990). Coaching from the margins: Issues in written response. In B. Kroll (Ed.), *Second language writing: Research insights for the classroom* (pp. 57–68). Cambridge, U.K.: Cambridge University Press.

Leki, I. (1992). *Understanding ESL writers.* Portsmouth, NH: Boynton/Cook.

Leki, I. (2001). A narrow thinking system: Nonnative-English-speaking students in group projects across the curriculum. *TESOL Quarterly, 35,* 39–67.

Leki, I., & Carson, J. (1997). "Completely different worlds": EAP and the writing experiences of ESL students in university courses. *TESOL Quarterly, 31*(1), 39–69.

Levinson, B. A., & Holland, D. (1996). The cultural production of the educated person: An introduction. In B. A. Levinson, D. E. Foley, & D. C. Holland (Eds.), *The cultural production of the educated person* (pp. 1–54). Albany: State University of New York Press.

Lisher, Linn. (2009). Personal interview. 29 December 2009.

Maloney, W.H. (2003). Connecting the texts of their lives to academic literacy: Creating success for at-risk first-year college students. *Journal of Adolescent & Adult Literacy, 46*(8), 664–673.

McCabe, R. (2000). Underprepared students. Measuring Up 2000: The State by State Report Card for Higher Education. San Jose, CA. Retrieved from http://measuringup.highereducation.org/2000/articles/UnderpreparedStudents.cfm

McGillin, V. A. (2003). Academic risk and resilience: Implications for advising at small colleges and universities. In M. K. Hemwall & K. C. Trachte (Eds.), *Advising and learning: Academic advising from the perspective of small colleges & universities.* NACADA: Manhattan, KS.

Miksch, K., Bruch, P., Higbee, J., Jehangir, R., & Lundell, D. (2003). The centrality of multiculturalism in developmental education. In J. L. Higbee, D. B. Lundell, & I. M. Duranczyk (Eds.), *Multiculturalism in developmental education* (pp. 5–13). Minneapolis: University of Minnesota, General College, Center for Research on Developmental Education and Urban Literacy.

Mohan, B. (1986). *Language and content.* Reading, MA: Addison-Wesley.

Muchinsky, D., & Tangren, N. (1999). Immigrant student performance in an academic intensive English program. In L. Harklau, K.M. Losey, & M. Siegal (Eds.), *Generation 1.5 meets college composition: Issues in teaching writing to U.S.-educated learners of ESL* (pp. 211–234). Mahwah, NJ: Lawrence Erlbaum.

Mulvey, M.E. (2008) Under-prepared students—A continuing challenge for higher education. *Research & Teaching in Developmental Education, 24*(2), 77.

Murie, R. (2001). *Generation 1.5 meets the freshman year: A case study of a college program.* 35th TESOL Convention, St. Louis, MO.

Murie, R., & Fitzpatrick, R. (2009). Situating generation 1.5 in the academy: Models for building academic literacy and acculturation. In M. Roberge, M. Siegal, & L. Harklau (Eds.), *Generation 1.5 in college composition: Teaching academic writing to U.S.-educated learners of ESL.* New York: Routledge.

Murie, R., & Thomson, R. (2001). When ESL is developmental: A model program for the freshman year. In J.L. Higbee (Ed.), *2001: A developmental odyssey* (pp. 15–28). Warrensburg, MO: National Association for Developmental Education.

Muuss, R.E. (1996). *Theories of adolescence.* New York: McGraw Hill.

National Clearinghouse of English Language Acquisition & Language Instruction Educational Programs. (2003).

National Council of Teachers of English (NCTE). (2008). *A nation with multiple languages.* Office of Policy Research. http://www.ncte.org

National Reading Panel. (2000). *Teaching students to read: An evidence based assessment of the scientific research literature on reading and its implications for reading instruction* [National Institute of Health Pub. No. 00-4769]. Washington, DC: National Institute of Child Health and Human Development.

National Research Council (NRC). (1999). *How people learn.* Washington DC: National Academy Press.

Nelson, B., Dunn, R., Griggs, S.A., Primavera, L., Fitzpatrick, M., & Bacilious, Z., et al. (1993). Effects of learning style intervention of college students' retention and achievement. *Journal of College Student Development, 34*(5), 364–369.

Notbohm, E. (2008). Gauging your teen's college readiness. *Children's VOICE, 17*(5), 22–23.

Novick, T.A. (2001). Praise for the five-paragraph essay. *The English Journal, 90*(3), 12.

Nunnally, T.E. (1991). Breaking the five-paragraph-theme barrier. *English Journal, 80*(1), 67–71.

Nuttall, G. (2005). Teaching vocabulary to generation 1.5 writers. Presentation at the 39th TESOL Convention, San Antonio, TX, March/April.

Oakes, J., Gamoran, A., & Page, R.N. (1992). Curriculum differentiation: Opportunities, outcomes, and meanings. In P.W. Jackson (Ed.), *Handbook of research on curriculum* (pp. 571–608). New York: Macmillan.

Ogbu, J. U. (1991). Low performance as an adaptation: The case of Blacks in Stockton, California. In M. A. Gibson & J. U. Ogbu (Eds.), *Minority status and schooling* (pp. 249–285). New York: Grand Publishing.

Ouellette, M.A. (2008). Weaving strands of writer identity: Self as author and the NNES "plagiarist." *Journal of Second Language Writing 17,* 255–273.

Patton, M. (2006). Generation 1.5 students: Introduction. DeAnza College Homepage. *Journal of Youth and Adolescence, 26,* 165–185.

Peacock, M. (2001). Match or mismatch? Learning styles and teaching styles in EFL. *International Journal of Applied Linguistics, 11*(1), 1–20.

Pecorari, D. (2003). Good and original: Plagiarism and patchwriting in academic second-language writing. *Journal of Second Language Writing, 12*(4), 317–345.

Pennycook, A. (1996). Borrowing others' words: Text, ownership, memory and plagiarism. *TESOL Quarterly, 30*(2), 201–230.

Peters, J. (2009). Engaging grammar lessons to give generation 1.5 writers a voice. CATESOL Conference. Pasadena, CA. April 17, 2009. Available at www.sfsu.edu/~lac/EngagingGrammarLessons.pdf

Pohan, C., & Kelly, N. (2004). Making content come alive for English learners: A student teacher's success story. *Action in Teacher Education, 25*(4), 58–64.

Porter, P., & van Dommelen, D. (2004). *Read, write, edit.* Boston: Houghton Mifflin.

Porter, P., & van Dommelen, D. (2005). Integrating assessment with grammar-for-writing instruction. 39th TESOL Convention, San Antonio, TX.

Raphan, C., & Moser, J. (1994). Linking language and content: ESL and art history. *TESOL Journal, 3*(2), 17–21.

Reid, J. (1997). Which non-native speaker? Differences between international students and U.S. resident (language minority) students. *New Directions for Teaching and Learning, 70,* 17–27.

Reynolds, D.W. (2009). *One on one with second language writers.* Ann Arbor: University of Michigan Press.

Roberge, M. (2002). California's generation 1.5 immigrants: What experiences, characteristics, and needs do they bring to our English classes? *The CATESOL Journal, 14*(1), 107–129.

Roberge, M. (2003). Academic literacy scaffolds for Generation 1.5 students. Paper presented at the 37th TESOL Convention, Baltimore, MD.

Roberge, M. (2009). A teacher's perspective on generation 1.5. In M. Roberge, M. Siegal, & L. Harklau (Eds.), *Generation 1.5 in college composition: Teaching academic writing to U.S.-educated learners of ESL.* New York: Routledge.

Roberts, N. (2003). *Instructor's manual/test bank to accompany Kelly/Lawton odyssey: A guide to better writing,* 3rd ed. New York: Longman.

Rochford, R.A. (2004). Improving academic performance and retention among remedial students. *The Community College Enterprise, 10*(2), 23–36.

Rosenshine, B., & Meister, C. (1992). The use of scaffolds for teaching higher level cognitive strategies. *Educational Leadership, 49*(7), 26–33.

Rumbaut, R. G., & Ima, K. (1988). *The adaption of Southeast Asian refugee youth: A comparative study. Final report to the Office of Resettlement.* (ERIC ED 299-372). San Diego: San Diego State University.

Sadek, C.S. (2008). Definition of "affective filter." *Educational Questions.* http://www.educational questions.com/qa47.htm

Samuels, S. (2002). Reading fluency: Its development and assessment. In S. Samuels & A. Farstrup (Eds.), *What research has to say about reading instruction,* 3rd ed. (pp. 166–183). Newark, DE: International Reading Association.

Schmidt, P. (2008). "Learning Community" programs can help at-risk students. *Chronicle of Higher Education.* July 3.

Schoem, D. (2005). *College knowledge: 101 Tips.* Ann Arbor: University of Michigan Press.

Schoenbach, R., Greenleaf, C., Cziko, C., & Hurwitz, L. (1999). *Reading for understanding: A guide to improving reading in middle and high school classrooms.* San Francisco: Jossey-Bass.

Segalowitz, N. (2000). Automaticity and attentional skill in fluent performance. In H. Riggenbach (Ed.), *Perspectives on fluency* (pp. 200–219). Ann Arbor: University of Michigan Press.

Shaughnessy, M. (1977). *Errors and expectations: A guide for the teacher of basic writing.* New York: Oxford University Press.

Sherman, J. (1992). Your own thoughts in your own words. *ELT Journal, 46*(2), 190–198.

Shi, L. (2004). Textual borrowing in second-language writing. *Written Communication, 21,* 171–200.

Shih, M. (1992). Beyond comprehension exercises in the ESL academic reading class. *TESOL Quarterly, 26*(2), 289–318.

Silberstein, S., Clarke, M.A., & Dobson, B.K. (2008). *Reader's Choice,* 5th ed. Ann Arbor: University of Michigan Press.

Silva, T. (1993). Toward an understanding of the distinct nature of L2 writing: The ESL research and its implications. *TESOL Quarterly, 27*(4), 657–677.

Skarin, R. (2001). Gender, ethnicity, class and social identity: A case study of two Japanese women in U.S. institutions. In E.F. Churchill & J.W. McLaughlin (Eds.), *Qualitative research in applied linguistics: Japanese learners and contexts* (pp. 26–65).Tokyo: Temple University Japan.

Sladky, L. (2010). One-third of students need remedial college math, reading. *USA Today,* May 11.

Smoke, T. (1988). Using feedback from ESL students to enhance their success in college. In S. Benesch (Ed.), *Ending remediation: Linking ESL and content in higher education* (pp. 7–19). Washington, DC: TESOL.

Spack, R. (1997). The acquisition of academic literacy in a second language: A longitudinal case study. *Written Communication, 14*(1), 3–62.

Spack, R. (2007). *Guidelines: A cross-cultural reading/writing text,* 3rd ed. New York: Cambridge University Press.

Spack, R. (2008). Teaching multilingual learners across the curriculum: An interactive plenary address. PennTESOL-East Spring Conference. Arcadia University.

Spanier, G. B. (2004). *Building on tradition to chart the future.* State of the University Address. Penn State University.

Spann, M.G. (2000). *Remediation: A must for the 21st century learning society.* Policy Paper, Denver, CO: Education Commission of the States.

Starks, G. (1989). Retention and developmental education: What the research has to say. *Research & Teaching in Developmental Education, 60*(1), 21–32.

Starr, L. (2000). "Scaffolding to success." Educational World®, http://www.education-world.com/a_curr/curr218.shtml

Stern, S. (2001). Learning assistance centers: Helping students through. ERIC-CC Digest, EDO-JC-01-07.

Stolarek, A. E. (1994). Prose modelling and metacognition: The effect of modeling on development of metacognition stance towards writing. *Research in the Teaching of English, 28,* 154–173.

Strole, C. (1997). Pedagogical responses from content faculty: Teaching content and language in history. In M.A. Snow & D.M. Brinton (Eds.), *The content-based classroom: Perspectives on integrating language and content* (pp. 104–116). White Plains, NY: Addison Wesley Longman.

Swan, M., & Smith, B. (2001). *Learner English: A teacher's guide to interference and other problems,* 2nd ed. New York: Cambridge.

Thonus, T. (2003). Serving generation 1.5 learners in the university writing center. *TESOL Journal, 12*(1), 17–24.

Tinto, V. (1998). Learning communities and the reconstruction of remedial education in higher education. Presented at the Conference on Replacing Remediation in Higher Education. Stanford University, January, 1998.

Tinto, V. (2004). *Student retention and graduation: facing the truth, living with the consequences.* The Pell Institute.

Tovani, C. (2000). *I read it, but I don't get it: Comprehension strategies for adolescent readers*. Portland, ME: Stenhouse.

Tritelli, D. (2003). From the editor, Association of American Colleges and Universities Peer Review. Winter issue. Retrieved from www.aacu.org/peerreview/pr-wi03/pr-wi03editor.cfm

Troutner, J. (2009). Bureau of education and research workshop. The radnor hotel, Radnor, PA. 4 November.

Urzua, C. (1987). "You stopped too soon": Second language children composing and revising. *TESOL Quarterly, 27*(2), 279–304.

Vygotsky, L.S. (1978). *Mind in society: The development of higher psychological processes*. Cambridge, MA: Harvard University Press.

Ward, M. (1997). Myths about college English as a second language. *Chronicle of Higher Education, 44*(5), B7–11.

Weissberg, R., & Hochhalter, G. L. (2006). Conversations in the writing center. In R. Weissberg, *Connecting speaking and writing in second language writing instruction* (pp. 76–98). Ann Arbor: University of Michigan Press.

Wesley, K. (2000). The ill-effects of the five-paragraph theme. *The English Journal, 90*(1), 57–60.

Williams, J. (1995). ESL composition program administration in the United States. *Journal of Second Language Writing, 4,* 157–179.

Williams, J. (2004). Tutoring and revision: Second language writers in the writing center. *Journal of Second Language Writing, 13*(3), 173–201.

Williams, J., & Snipper, G.C. (1990). *Literacy and bilingualism*. New York: Longman.

Winkler, A.C., & McCuen-Wetherell, J.R. (2003). *Writing talk*, 3rd ed. Upper Saddle River, NJ: Prentice Hall.

Yamada, K. (2003). What prevents ESL/EFL writers from avoiding plagiarism?: Analyses of 10 North-American college websites. *System, 31*(2), 247–258.

Yoon, H., & Hirvela, A. (2004). ESL student attitudes toward corpus use in L2 writing. *Journal of Second Language Writing, 13*(4), 257–283.

Zamel, V. (1991). Acquiring language, literacy, and academic discourse: Entering ever new conversations. *College ESL, 1*(1), 10–18.

Zamel, V. (1995). Strangers in academia: The experiences of faculty and ESL students across the curriculum. *College Composition and Communication, 46*(4), 506–521.

Zhang, Z. (1994). The development and use of a reading strategy inventory for ESL college students. Paper presented at the Annual Meeting of the Mid-South Educational Research Association. Nashville, TN. November 9–11. ED 382 920.